Werewolves

Werewolves

A Field Guide to Shapeshifters, Lycanthropes, and Man-Beasts

By Dr. Bob Curran

New Page Books
A Division of The Career Press, Inc.
Franklin Lakes, N.J.

WEREWOLVES
EDITED AND TYPESET BY GINA TALUCCI
Cover design by Lucia Rossman/DigiDog Design
Printed in the U.S.A. by Courier

To order this title, please call toll-free 1-800-CAREER-1 (NJ and Canada: 201-848-0310) to order using VISA or MasterCard, or for further information on books from Career Press.

The Career Press, Inc., 3 Tice Road, PO Box 687,
Franklin Lakes, NJ 07417
www.careerpress.com
www.newpagebooks.com

Library of Congress Cataloging-in-Publication Data

Curran, Bob.
  Werewolves : a field guide to shapeshifters, lycanthropes and man-beasts / by Bob Curran.
    p. cm.
  Includes index.
  ISBN 978-1-60163-089-6
    1. Werewolves. I. Title.

GR830.W4C87 2009
398.24'54--dc22

                                                                2009025581

Contents

Introduction

A Walk on the Wild Side

7

Chapter 1

The Shadow of the Wolf

17

Chapter 2

Man Into Beast

53

Chapter 3
Old Irish Wolves and Other Wonders
93

Chapter 4
The French Connection
135

Chapter 5
Barking Mad
167

Conclusion
Fangs Ain't What They Used to Be
203

Bibliography
215

Index
219

About the Author
223

Introduction: A Walk on the Wild Side

Somewhere among the shadows which throng the deepest recesses of the human mind, a ferocious beast is crouching. This is something extremely ancient and primal—a relic of mankind's original history, a fragment of his initial, bestial nature. Although the eons have left a veneer of civilization and culture on us, the beast still waits deep within every one of us, ready to emerge at any time if the conditions are right, to create mayhem, and even death, all around it.

That at least is the theory, both psychological and supernatural, which is sometimes used to explain grotesque or violent behavior in humans. It has also formed the basis of many films, whether they be psychological dramas or straight monster movies, which have both horrified and thrilled us throughout the years. Is this because we instinctively recognize the creature that lurks somewhere beneath the surface of our own sophistication?

In Western culture, arguably, nothing has come to symbolize the idea of the ancient beast lurking within the human psyche better than the concept of the werewolf. In the cinema and books this idea is often portrayed as a civilized person who is transformed into a ravening wolf or wolf-like creature perhaps under the baleful influence of the moon's rays. Indeed, such a concept is so deeply ingrained into our culture that the prefix *were* is generally suggestive of a human who can transform him- or herself into an often ferocious animal and do harm against his or her neighbors—as in were-leopard, were-bear, or were-wolf. But where does the concept and word come from, and how has it become so deeply rooted in our consciousness? The answer is perhaps more complex than we might imagine.

The prefix *were, wher,* or *wehr* is undoubtedly of Saxon, Germanic, or Viking origin (deriving perhaps from the Old Norse *vargr*, meaning outlaw or wild man, or the Germanic *wagr,* although this is only a suggestion), and is usually taken to mean man, although its strict interpretation may not have anything to do with persons turning into animals or even adopting animal characteristics. In an early form of Norse law, for example, there was a concept of *weregild* or *weregelt*, which was a form of compensation paid to an individual's family or community for his or her unlawful slaying. Such a killing might have been in battle, by accident, or, in some cases, as murder, and the law had worked out a strict system whereby family or community might be recompensed. The phrase of course meant "man money" or "person money," and was enshrined in the early laws of a number of northern countries where compensation seems to have been paid to a number of nobles' families (the payment only applied to those of reasonably high status) who had members killed in localized conflicts.

There is no reference to the prefix being linked with the word *wolf* or *wulf* until the 11th century, when it appears in England as a personal name. In fact it is thought to have been an addition to the name Wulfstan (roughly translated as "wolf stone"), a name that applied to several English churchmen around the 11th century in order to denote rank or status. Very crudely translated it may mean "the man," suggesting greatness and invincibility at a time when much of England and its churches were under Viking attack. The most famous bearer of the title was Wulfstan II (died May 1023), Bishop of London and Worcester, and Archbishop of York. He is named as one of the successors of Wulfstan I (died December 26th, 956) and *may* be related in some way to St. Wulfstan (1008–1087), another Bishop of Worcester and a Christian saint. In fact, his name may not have been Wulfstan at all, but one that he took in deference to his predecessor. When Wolfstan II was ordained as Bishop of London in 996, he also took the personal title of "Lupus" (wolf or dog), styling himself "the Wolf Bishop." He would later sign his correspondence with the title "Lupus Episcupus," which earned him the nickname "Bishop Wehrwolf." There is no doubt that Wulfstan was an important and valiant churchman—he needed to be. These were turbulent times both for England and the English Church, with repeated Viking invasions and the establishment of powerful Viking kingdoms, especially in the north of the country.

In 1002, Wulfstan took over the Episcopal See of Worcester and also the Archbishopic of York, becoming Lord Archbishop (the first churchman to be dually elected). York had always been contentious in Viking times, because Wulfstan I had aided the vicious Norse Jarl of Orkney, Erik Bloodaxe, to seize the kingdom of Northumbria, and had established himself in the Norse kingdom of Jorvik in which York lay (and which also gave the city its name).

The election of Wulfstan II as a powerful churchman firmed up the Church's hold on that turbulent area and his rule firmly established Christianity there. There is no doubt that he was instrumental in the restructuring of the early English Church, bringing in what became known as the Benedictine Reform, which had emerged in Europe during the Carolingian Empire.

This sought to impose monastic standards of piety of local clergy and to modify lax church behavior. From his exalted position, Wulfstan was able to enforce this. He pressed for church reform through a series of extremely strident homilies, which were directed to all churches within his large episcopate. One of these (written around 997 when he was Bishop of London) is entitled *Sermo Lupis ad Anglos* (*the Sermon of the Wolf to the English*) and rails against moral laxity in the country as a whole. This text is widely regarded as his most famous and also his most vitriolic. So great a policy-maker and administrator was Wulfstan that he became the official law-maker (secular and religious) for two English kings—Aethelred II (Ethelred the Unready 978–1013 and 1014–1016) and the Viking ruler Canute the Great (1016–1035). There seems to be little doubt that Wulfstan was one of the most powerful law-makers in England and was deserving of the title "Archbishop Werewolf" to signal his importance. There may also have been another reason for the nickname.

Wulfstan was widely renowned across England for his homilies, most of which were little more than ferocious and venomous attacks on the laws laid down by his predecessors and on the then current practices within the Church, which Wulfstan did not consider as reflecting true piety. In an era when the line between the sacred and the secular was often blurred (his predecessor Wulfstan I had tried to become both spiritual and secular ruler of Northumbria) and corruption in the Church was widespread, such virulent criticism was

considered necessary in order to bring about reform, and the often irascible Wulfstan II seemed the man to do it. Many of his homilies were extremely savage in tone—indeed, a block of them written at the end of the 10th century are known as "The Black Days" segment. (Similar to many churchmen of his time, Wulfstan assumed that the world would end in fire and pestilence in the year 1000, and God would smite the wicked and usher in a reign of holiness for the rest of eternity.) Coupled with such ferociousness, the fact that he styled himself "the Wolf Bishop" conjures up images of a wolf viciously attacking the populace, and added strength to such condemnation. In this case, the term *wehrwolf* (man-wolf) may well have been considered extremely apposite.

But the term *wehr* or even *wulf* (which Wulfstan himself may well have adopted) was not solely confined to forceful churchmen. It was believed among some of the early peoples that adding the name of a wolf or hound to a person's name would make him valiant and strong, as well as signifying greatness and ferocity. Great leaders and warriors were often anxious to make this addition to their given names. Thus, the Irish adopted the prefix *cu* (meaning hound), placing it in front of the names of some of their chiefs and heroes. Thus we find the hero Cu-Cuhullain (the Hound of Ulster) and the king Cu-Roi (Cu-Ri—the Hound King) appearing in Irish legend. Similarly, both the Norse and Saxons adopted either the prefix or suffix *wulf* to denote strength and ferocity—for example Eadwulf—and this may be why Wulfstan may be an adoptive name as previously mentioned. The idea of a man-wolf may not then initially have referred to a shapeshifter or to an unwilling victim in the grip of a demonic spirit, but, as we shall see later, to a strong leader or mighty warrior. The term *wahr* was also incorporated into personalized names, and may have become a name itself in the English surname Ware. This too signified a warrior and commanded respect.

Introduction

Although the word *werewolf* was used to describe himself and to describe his status and authority by Archbishop Wulfstan (he did not coin the phrase and it may have been used before him), the next authenticated reference, also set in a Church context, shifted the emphasis of the word a little differently. This was *The History and Topography of Wales* written around 1182 by Geraldus Cembrensius (Gerald of Wales), a respected monk who had acted as Confessor to Prince John, one of the sons of the English King Henry II. In this text, Geraldus tells of Welsh King Vereticus, who was turned into a wolf by the Irish Saint Patrick. According to one old legend, Vereticus had led a Welsh raid into Ireland and had occupied a small part of the country, and the saint had come to drive him out. Vereticus was considered to be extremely barbaric and ferocious in his ways, and so Patrick changed him into the animal that he most resembled—that is, a wolf. The legend was at one time current in both Ireland and Wales, which is where Geraldus recorded it. In some ways it shows the status and ferocity of Vereticus, but the tale— gullibly repeated as history by Geraldus—also demonstrates the power of the Church in an era when that institution was trying to establish itself over secular concerns. The underlying message was that the king must now become subservient to the power of the holy man, even though he kept his ferocity and strength.

Nor was St. Patrick the only Celtic saint to achieve this transformation; Saint Natalis was able to turn an entire clan into wolves because of an ancient sin. And there were supposedly others whose exploits appear in Christian legend throughout Ireland, Scotland, and Wales. The idea of the werewolf— the man into animal—which, as we shall see, had lain just below the surface of human consciousness, was now taking on a specific form in social thinking, and the foundations of our modern image of the creature were being laid. But it was not only within a Church context that the beast appeared—secular society was taking note as well.

Werewolves

Writing in his text *Otia Imperia* (*Resurrection of the Emperor*) around 1212, the medieval chronicler Gervase of Tilbury (1150–1218) makes mention of a man who transformed himself into the guise of a wolf by rolling naked in sand for a long period of time. He also interestingly suggests that such transformations might be linked to the full moon, although this was not a common medieval belief, has appeared recently in more modern books and films. A churchman named Gervase also moved in the secular world (he was a legal expert on canon law) and appeared regularly at the Imperial court. His patron was the Holy Roman Emperor, Otto IV, for whom the *Otia Imperia* was written and to whom it was dedicated; this gives a clue as to Gervase's impressive standing at the Emperor's court. The text falls into the genre of what became known as *speculum literature*—taking its name from the magic mirror or *speculum*, which both wizards and holy men were believed to possess. The mirror showed them what was happening elsewhere in the world, which was supposed to be an encyclopaedic and knowledgeable compendium of the matters to which it addressed itself. Gervase's book was supposed to be a complete and informed collection of the wonders of the world and was to be treated as fact. Thus, given Gervase's undoubted learning and status among his peers, the idea of a man changing into a wolf was readily accepted, both by the Emperor and his subjects.

Other courtiers began to write about men turning into wild creatures both in text and poem. These circulated widely not only at the Emperor's court, but at the French and English courts as well. And from the court and the Church, the perception began to trickle down to the common people. The notion of a man turning into a wild beast and back again was taking a hold on the human mind. This pattern would continue down through the centuries, arguably, as we shall discuss later, reaching a peak in France around the 16th and 17th centuries. And of course, the idea of the beast—the savage, ancient enemy—

has continued to haunt the human psyche even into the present day, prowling just beneath the veneer that we are pleased to call society.

But what are the actual origins of this belief, and why does it fill us so much with dread? The idea of the werewolf may represent an amalgam of a number of deep human fears and perceptions—the separation from nature, the fear of the wild, a horror of cannibalism, and an inherent awareness of the savagery and ferocity that often lies under the veneer of human "civilization." The howl of the wolf, suggestive of loneliness and vulnerability, has come to symbolize this coalition of deep feelings in a most potent way, and the fear that we ourselves can and might turn into such a creature therefore becomes arguably our worst and most ancient nightmare. So let's explore these terrifying pathways and see if we can tease out the origins of the werewolf legend. Let's go wolf hunting!

1
The Shadow
of the Wolf

Speak of the wolf and you'll see his fangs.

—Old Irish Proverb

Arguably, the wolf is mankind's oldest foe, with an enmity that goes back almost into pre-human times. It was with the wolf that our distant ancestors competed for game and with whom they probably fought in the primal forests of an early world. And it may also be that the wolf won over the proto-men, for they were quick, strong and cunning, probably more able to chase and hunt down food than our heavy and

lumbering forebears and even better at defending their territory than the early men. It had four legs, which gave it added speed, a sleek, lithe body that leant itself to the chase, and sharp, ripping teeth which could tear its quarry open in the merest hint of time. In every way, it seemed to be a fearsome and successful hunting and killing machine, better than anything our ancient ancestors could produce. Is it any wonder then, that early man both hated and feared the wolf? And yet, there was much to admire about the animal, for the very things that made mankind fear it also appealed to early men. They envied its strength and ferocity, its sleekness and speed, its tirelessness and hunting prowess. In many respects, the wolf was the enemy they often wished they could emulate. In a world where the distinction between humans and beasts was usually blurred, these attributes were normally vital for survival, and our ancestors probably longed to be as successful a hunter as the wolf.

Perhaps almost as an extension of that wish, the attributes of man and animal began to meld and flow together in the human mind. Perhaps if the man could ape the wolf in all its attributes, he would somehow acquire at least some of the creature's prowess and superior hunting skills. But how could men achieve such skills? The answer, in part, lay in supernatural means. By using the powers of another world, where perhaps animalistic spirits reigned supreme, humans could perhaps induce in themselves the wolf-like strength, cunning, swiftness, and aggression that they themselves seemed to lack. The wolf, of course, was among a pantheon of other animals with which early humans shared the world and which they also seemed to admire, but it seems to be one of the most predominant creatures whose skills were considered worth acquiring. This indeed marked its undoubted status as a hunter.

Hunting, in those early times, must have been an extremely precarious and difficult element in the survival of a human community. In pre-agricultural times, a lack of prey captured and killed by hunters meant starvation and ultimately extinction for the ever-expanding groups of early peoples—it was the difference between life and death in a very real sense. This was particularly true in the long, harsh winters when game was scarce and the wolves often proved much more adaptable than the knots of humans who kept close to the fires out of the cold. It was at such a time that feral attributes truly came into their own and that mankind wished it was more like the wolf. Perhaps, if men actually *pretended* to be wolves, they might acquire or draw down some of the characteristics needed for survival in difficult times. If they wrapped themselves in wolf skins and adopted a wolf-like posture, perhaps the nature spirits would mistake them for actual wolves and bestow the required skills and strengths on them. But in order to confer such an animus upon the hunters, a supernatural liaison in the form of a shaman had to contact the appropriate spirits. This shaman may well have *appeared* animal-like.

The Sorcerer

The earliest representation as to how such a shaman might have looked has come down to us from France. This is the celebrated figure known as "Sorcerer de Trois Freres"—a remarkable Palaeolithic drawing found on the wall of a cave system deep beneath the Pyrenees in the Montesquieu-Avantes region. The so-called "Sorcerer" (the figure is taken to represent an early shaman) is depicted as a curious creature—a hybrid combining elements of both the human and animal. The drawing appears to catch him in some sort of dancing posture, moving sideways and upward on two human feet, but slouching forward as if ready to drop onto all fours like an animal, balancing himself on bear-like forepaws. Large antlers adorn his forehead above a bearded human-like face from which intelligent eyes stare owlishly out. But at his hindquarters, a bushy wolf-like tail can clearly be seen, swinging back to reveal a lion-like phallus.

The cavern in which the painting has been created can only be approached by crawling almost horizontally along a connecting tunnel of about 30 or 40 yards, and cultural historians such as Joseph Campbell have suggested that the awkward near-inaccessibility of the site served to give it an air of mystery and mysticism. The Sorcerer is indeed a strange and enigmatic figure, and it is not hard to imagine the drawing at the very heart of some distant Palaeolithic worship. The drawing has been dated to around 13,000 BC, which led cultural anthropologists such as Margaret Murray to (perhaps erroneously) claim that this was a depiction of "one of the first gods on earth." Another archaeologist and anthropologist, the Frenchman Henri Breuil (1877–1961), who incidentally had originally discovered and sketched the painting, disagreed and described the representation probably as a shaman in the form of a "therianthrope" (an idealized figure combining both human and animal characteristics). Later speculation suggested that they were both wrong, and has suggested that the drawing was that of a shaman of the Magadalinan culture, which existed at the end of the last great European ice age, around 10,000 BC. Many learned speculations, however, have connected the figure with some sort of hunting ritual and say that it is suggestive of humans taking on the attributes of their prey or quarry. The linkage of the human and animal worlds in this activity is unmistakable.

Although nothing is written about the Sorcerer or even about the hunting practices he may have embodied (he existed in a time long before writing), it is suggested that the wolf may have formed a significant part of his figure. Wolves may have attracted much of early man's attention, for, although probably implacable enemies, the two also shared certain characteristics. Similar to ancient men, wolves were social animals. They hunted in packs, they obeyed strict laws of leadership, and they cared for their young. Indeed, these were also human characteristics, and it is therefore not surprising that they formed the foundation of a perceptual bond between humans and wolves. The perception of such a bond formed the basis of a few very ancient legends. It was said, for example, that wolves might raise abandoned human children as their own (a theme that we shall return to later in the book).

Romulus and Remus

According to ancient tradition, for example, the founders of the eternal city of Rome, Romulus and Remus (771–717 BC and 771–753 BC respectively) were supposed to have been suckled and raised by a kindly she-wolf. The twins, reputedly the sons of the war god Mars, were abandoned as small infants by their mother Rhea Silvia, a vestal virgin, in the area of Alba Longa (supposedly situated around the modern day Alban Hills) in the territory of ancient Latium, and were left to die in a swamp. They were discovered by a foraging she-wolf who viewed them with an almost human compassion. According to some variations of the legend, the wolf was the embodiment of the wolf goddess Luperca, which seems to suggest that there was a highly developed system of wolf-worship among the early Latins. Whoever or whatever she was, the she-wolf looked after the infants, suckling them with her own milk, until they were subsequently found by the shepherd Faustulus, who raised them as his own sons. Later they would find out their true identity and would be called by the people of Latium to find and rule a major city following the death of their uncle and former king, Amulius. Romulus would later kill Remus (according to some it was in a wolf-like frenzy, culminating in a blow to Remus's head with a spade) to become the first king of Rome. Imbedded within this tale is an idea of union between man and beast—the she-wolf suckled two young human children as she would her own cubs—and perhaps this forms part of the legendary juxtaposition of man and wolf.

Gilgamesh

Old though the story of Romulus and Remus might be, it is certainly not the oldest known story concerning men and wolves. Indeed, perhaps the most ancient tale comes from the second millennium BC and involves an actual transformation into an animal. The celebrated *Epic of Gilgamesh* is one of the oldest existing texts that we know about, and was originally written for the ancient Kings of Uruk (later Mesopotamia), later being translated into Akkadian. It tells of the exploits of Gilgamesh, a god-king and son of Lugalbanda, the fifth king of the first dynasty, who supposedly reigned around 2,600 BC. The *Epic* was little more than a collection of ancient oral tales put into some form of order for the amusement and delectation of the court, and also to give both status and glory to its former kings. Gilgamesh was supposedly loved by the goddess Ishtar, who made advances toward him. The hero, however, rejected her because of her treatment of former suitors. A young shepherd had also fallen in love with the goddess some time before and made copious offerings to her at a shrine on a mountainside. At first, the vain Ishtar encouraged him, but, being the capricious entity she was, she soon tired of his devotions and turned him into the guise of a wolf. He was then torn to pieces by his own hounds. This ancient story may have formed the basis for the later Greek myth of the hunter Actaeon—the most famous hunter in all of the Greek states—who surreptitiously spied on the goddess Artemis as she bathed in a woodland pool. Discovering what he had done, the goddess became enraged and turned the hapless Actaeon into the form of a stag; similar to the shepherd, he too was torn to shreds by his own hounds.

Niciros

Although the Gilgamesh story is often cited as the most ancient recorded werewolf story available, some scholars dismiss it as not being an actual werewolf tale, saying that no actual transformation occurs within the tale. They point instead to a detail in the *Satyricon,* a work written by the Roman writer Petronius (AD 27–66), a scribe at the court of the Emperor Nero. The work was written around AD 61, but was not published until 1664 when it was only sporadically circulated. It details the escapades of two homosexual friends—Encolpius and Gita—but also contains the story of Niciros, a soldier who traveled with an acquaintance to a distant city. On their journey, they stopped off in a deserted graveyard to relieve themselves. To the soldier's horror, his companion, with an evil laugh, made a circle of urine around himself, threw off his clothes (which turned to stone), changed into the guise of a wolf, and bounded off to do harm in a neighboring settlement. There, he was wounded in the throat by a spear wielded by one of the populace and was forced to flee; Niciros was treated for the wound in a nearby house. There are, of course, many subtexts in the tale—to urinate within the precincts of a grave-yard was an insult to the dead and would invite some sort of supernatural consequences. Also, the idea that the companion might turn into a ravening wolf shows how much ancient perceptions of the animal persisted even into classical times.

Lykaon Legends

Indeed, the wolf still featured largely as a creature of both terror and admiration throughout the ancient world. In classical Greece, for example, there was the mysterious ritual on the top of Mount Lykaon, a remote spot in the highlands of Arcadia in the Peloponnesus peninsula. Mention of this place and of the clandestine rituals that went on there comes down to us from the

Greek writer Pausanius (a Lydian geographer who died in the kingdom of Sparta somewhere between 470 and 465 BC). At the time of his writing, the lower slopes of the mountain were covered by thick forests, which were the home of predatory wolves, making it a most dangerous area indeed. The upper slopes, however, were bare and rocky, and the boulders there were said to conceal a strange shrine dedicated to the Lykaian Zeus, where strange rites were carried out. The name given to the mountain has its origins in ancient Greek legend. Lykaon was originally said to have been a person—a prehistoric king, in fact, who ruled Arcadia in the years before the Great Deluge. In an attempt to ingratiate himself with the god Zeus, the king invited the deity to a feast on the high mountainside at which he served up human flesh—said by some versions of the story to be that of his own son, Nyktimos, or of his nephew Arkas. When Zeus found that he'd been eating human flesh, he was outraged and in a fit of anger turned Lykaon into a wolf. The transformation would last nine years, after which Lykaon would turn back into a man, provided he had not tasted human flesh while in the wolf guise. If he had eaten human flesh, he would remain a wolf forever. The ritual at which Pausanius hinted possibly involved the worship of Zeus in the guise of a wolf. This led some writers to assume that it may have involved human sacrifice and cannibalism.

However, the Greek cultural writer Walter Burkert, basing his theory on the writings of Pliny, suggests that the ritual may have been a kind of "rite of passage" practiced by young males in certain Arcadian communities or families. Pliny suggests that a young man was chosen from among the family and taken to a remote spot, where he hung his clothes on an oak tree, swam across a lake, and went into the wild to live like a wolf for nine years, whereupon he swam back, dressed himself, and resumed his human life as a full-grown man. In those nine years, he was not to have tasted human flesh, else he become a beast of the forest and beyond humanity. The notion of the swimming across water is significant, as it suggests, according to cultural anthropologists, a break with the human world. There may, of course, have also been some sort of human sacrifice involved, but the exact nature of this is unclear. Although not doubting this, Pausanius is extremely sceptical of the metamorphosis of human into wolf.

Damarchus

He does, however, mention another connected story (the exact veracity of which he also doubts) concerning an Arcadian boxer named Damarchus, who was a champion of the Olympic Games around 400 BC. He competed after having been changed into a wolf and back to human form again nine years later. However, many other Greek writers were not so skeptical as Pausanius—Arcadia was, after all, a geographically enclosed and often mysterious place usually associated with the supernatural and witchcraft. His skill and prowess were, of course, linked to the fact that he was in some way connected to a wolf.

Worshipping of the Gods

But boxers were not the only martial wolves of the ancient world. Pliny also states that at the foot of Mount Soracte in Eturia, Italy, roughly 26 miles from Rome, a peculiar ceremony was carried out once a year in honor of the goddess Feronia. She seems to have been some sort of fertility goddess, sacred to growing plants and to some species of animal—although these are not exactly specified. The festival was known as that of the *Hirpi Sorani* or of the Soranian Wolves, and drew large crowds, not only from all the surrounding villages, but also from the city of Rome. During the festival certain men, known as Wolf Wizards or Wolf Soldiers, who were possessed by the spirits of wolves, would walk barefoot across burning coals without any apparent harm. As a consequence of this act, they were exempted by the civil authorities from any sort of public service or duty, and were held in high esteem by the populace. These men were considered to be invincible and performed great feats of strength and daring at a carnival associated with the event, still under the possession of the wolf spirits.

There was much debate among ancient writers as to whether this ritual was conducted in honor of the goddess Feronia at all. Pliny and Virgil argued that this formed part of a much older form of worship, which long pre-dated the goddess, directed toward the god of the mountain whose name was Soranus. This was later changed into the name of the god Apollo, although there is a suggestion that in his original form, Soranus may have appeared in the guise of a wolf. Another Roman writer and follower of Livy and Virgil, Silus Italicus (AD 25 or 26–1017) speaks of men passing through fire following a human sacrifice, carrying human entrails in their hands—this act conferring on them a supernatural "touch" and giving them the status of "wizards." Whether this is at the festival of Feronia at Mount Soracte, however, is unclear.

Neuri

Some classical writers sweepingly attached the brand of werewolfery to certain races of men. The venerable Herodotus (484–425 BC), for example, declared in *Histories* that some members of the Neuri, a tribe living on the borders of Scythia (modern Ukraine) changed into the form of wolves for a period, and, at the very least, the tribe were anthropophagi (eaters of men in the original meaning of the word). Although it might have been true that some Neuri were cannibals, there is little to suggest that they adopted the guise of wolves or that the wolf was an especially important creature among them. The

story may well have been no more than the result of xenophobia among neighbouring races, but there may have been a grain of truth, perhaps with regard to cannibalism.

Anubis

The Greeks and Romans were, of course, not the only ancient peoples to venerate gods associated with dogs or wolves. The Egyptians too worshipped deities that boasted both human bodies and the heads of wild wolf-like creatures. The best known is, of course, Anubis, possibly an early Egyptian god of the dead, but later the deity who oversaw the embalming and mummification processes. This deity was a hybrid entity, with the head of a desert jackal and the body of a human being, its flesh sometimes dark and rotting. Sometimes, however, he was shown in full canine form. The cult of Anubis flourished in Egypt during the period which archaeologists call "the Old Kingdom" (third millennium BC), but worship of the god may well have been older than that. He would later be replaced in mythology by Osiris, who had reputedly been resurrected and had thus conquered death. During the Old Kingdom, Anubis was one of eight gods (the Ogdoad) who were believed to rule the country around the Nile. Perhaps he is best known for his depiction in the celebrated Egyptian *Book of the Dead* weighing the hearts of the dead on a scale to determine worthiness to enter the Afterlife. There is little doubt that, because he was a kind of gatekeeper between one world and another, Anubis was an extremely important deity to the ancient Egyptians. The doghead and his association with the dead is probably based on the jackal, a scavenger who haunted graveyards and who was linked to digging up and devouring dead corpses.

Wepwawet

It has already been noted that despite his great antiquity, Anubis may have been the later embodiment of an older deity. A prime contender for this is Wepwawet, a deity associated with the city of Asyut in Upper Egypt, later named Lycopolis (the City of Wolves) in the Graeco-Roman period. Similar to Anubis (with whom he is often confused), Wepwawet is sometimes depicted as a man with the head of a wolf or jackal, but more often as a wolf (hence the Greek name for his city). He was regarded as the Opener of the Way—the deity who guided the souls of the dead through Duat (a region in Egyptian belief that resembled the early Christian idea of purgatory) and was also regarded as extremely fierce. It may be that Wepwawet was actually the representation of a pharaoh (or perhaps several pharaohs) of the Old Kingdom who wished to have wolf-like characteristics attributed to them. For this reason, the god was often considered a "champion of royalty" and something of a war deity. A tablet from Sinai states that Wepwawet "opened the way" for the "great victory" of King Sekhemket (a pharaoh of the third dynasty), over his enemies, which suggests that the pharaoh may have been aggressive (wolf-like) in battle. Depictions of the god show him in Egyptian military dress and carrying either a bow or a mace, both suggestive of his ferocity. In some cases, he is depicted as carrying the mace of King Nermar, an Egyptian pharaoh who reigned in the 31st century BC, as a symbol of his great antiquity (and, by association, the antiquity of the wolf cult in Ancient Egypt). Later, as Wepwawet became assimilated into the traditional Egyptian pantheon, he became portrayed as the son of Anubis (perhaps because of his visual resemblance to that god), although some traditions describe him as the son of the serpent god Set.

Fenrir

Wolf gods were certainly not confined to the classical world or to ancient Egypt. In the frozen Scandinavian northlands where wolves dominated, it is not surprising to find that they found their way into Norse mythology or that, as deities, they were incredibly fierce and bad-tempered. The most famous of all the Nordic wolf-gods was Fenrir—sometimes rendered as Fenris (in some versions, he is described as a "wolf-demon" to distinguish him from the "true" gods of Asgard), the eldest son of the Norse god Loki (the god of mischief and of evil), and the giantess Angroboda (whose name means "herald of sorrow"). He was a monster in the form of a gigantic wolf whom the gods had learned from a prophesy would one day bring about Ragnarok, the end of all things. However, when he was a cub, he posed little threat, but the cub grew and became a monster. The gods decided that he should be chained up, but by now the wolf was so strong that it broke every chain that was placed on it. It looked as though it would bring the end of the universe, and something drastic needed to be done. They instructed the dwarves to make something that would hold Fenrir, so a material called Gleipnir was created in the forges under the earth. This was a substance that was extremely soft and yet could not be broken. It was made from a number of unusual elements—the beard of a woman, the roots of a mountain, the footstep of a cat, the breath of fishes, the sinews of a bear, and the spittle of birds. With this, the gods hoped to bind the monster so that he couldn't escape. Fenrir, however, was extremely wary, and although the gods invited him to a grand feast, he refused to be bound by such a weak-looking substance. After much haggling, he agreed, provided one of the gods would place his or her hand between his jaws. Many of the gods refused to do so, but the god Tyr or Tiw (after whom Tuesday is named) agreed. Fenrir was bound by the Gleipnir, and though he struggled mightily, he could not break free. In anger and frustration, he bit off Tiw's hand, but he still could not escape. The gods chained him to a rock called Gioll somewhere in the underworld, forcing a sword between his jaws to keep him from biting anyone. There he waited for Ragnarok, the end of all things.

As the eons passed the Gleipnir weakened, and when Ragnarok arrived, Fenrir burst free and attacked the gods once more, slaying Odin and bringing about the end of the universe as was prophesied. He was eventually killed by one of Odin's sons—Vidar, the second strongest of all the gods—but not in time to save all things. In the Viking mind, Fenrir represented two of the strongest (and often interconnected) elements that sometimes characterized Norse life: strength and the fear of destruction.

Although Fenrir appears in what we might describe as standardized Norse myth, he is probably an amalgam of the beliefs of localized wolf cults across the Scandinavian world. Wolf packs prowled the forests of Norway, Denmark, and many other countries, and wolf spirits were worshipped in many villages and communities all across the land. These were not only aggressive entities, but also protective and beneficial guardians, as well. In fact, in the depths of winter they sometimes rewarded those who had faithfully worshipped them all year—becoming almost a prototype for the modern-day Santa Claus! As well as becoming a symbol of power and strength, the wolf had also become a symbol of protection and good fortune for the community.

Native American Beliefs

The idea of the wolf as a protective spirit or totem was, of course, not unique to Norse culture; it was to be found among such civilizations as the Native American. A number of Native tribes had adopted the wolf as their totem and continue to hold it as such right up to the present day. The Indians viewed the wolf in a rather different way than western Europe. They viewed the creature as a fellow hunter whom they both respected and admired. They envied its cunning, ferocity, boundless energy, and speed—what better protector could their tribe have to look after it? In a number of Indian legends, the wolf appears as a protector, particularly of the weak and defenseless members of the community. In Shoshone folklore, for example, the wolf is always the protector of women and of young children. In an old tale, a Shoshone village was attacked by raiders with a group of small children—mainly girls— and some of their mothers escape into the surrounding forests. They were pursued by their enemies, who were bent on the extermination of the entire community. Hiding in the undergrowth, they met with a pack of wolves, and, rather than attack them, the animals formed a protective ring around them and drove off their enemies with sharp fangs. Later, the fugitives were able to return and rebuild their community, thanks to the wolves. Thereafter, the wolf became the totem of the village.

In the frozen north, where the animals abounded, the wolf also became a totem, particularly of the Tingit tribe, fur traders in Northern Alaska. Indeed, a spectacularly carved, fierce-looking wooden wolf adorned the grave of a Tingit chieftain in Wragnell, Alaska, presumably to keep desecrators and defilers away. Representations of the wolf spirit also appear in various Indian totem poles still to be seen in a number of Alaskan and Canadian towns and villages.

Supernatural Experiences

Indian lore viewed the wolf as exceptionally wise, especially in supernatural matters. In fact, as well as being a protector of a community, the creature became something of a counselor to certain individuals within it—particularly to young men during their rites of passage within the tribe or village, such as the transition from boyhood to manhood. In dreams, the wolf would act as a form of "spirit guide" leading them through the various difficult pathways into adulthood—for example, becoming a hunter—and offering advice and sage counsel along the way. Local shamans, who sometimes officiated during rituals at such times, often wore wolf pelts and wolf heads to symbolize their connection to the deity. In some cases, they also adopted animal-like characteristics in order to draw the spirits to them, so that they might consult with them. In effect, these shamans almost took on the aspect of wolves as part of their ritual—giving a localized perspective to the man-wolf legend. As the shaman became connected to the wolf spirits, he became a wolf in a supernatural manner. He was *transformed* into the beast—snapping, growling, and clawing—so that he might guide his protégés within the community. He was in fact the very *essence* of the werewolf, as we might understand it. And, most probably, the wolf-priests of other cultures may well have adopted the same attributes, laying the very foundation for the werewolf legend in the popular mind—the man changed into a beast by supernatural means. The image would leave an indelible impression in the human psyche.

Christianity

It was not long before the developing Christian Church also adopted the imagery of the wolf in some of its legends. Several saints were depicted with having either wolf heads or exhibiting wolf-like characteristics, which became the stuff of Christian fable, and saints sometimes changed from men into hounds and vice versa. One such story concerned the 13th-century story of the French saint Guinefort, who was linked to an early holy man. According to tradition, it was said that the saint had been born as a greyhound, which was the pet of a wealthy nobleman. This lord had a young infant son whom the dog was supposed to guard against harm. One day after returning from a hunting trip the noble found the infant's crib and the infant covered in blood. There was also blood around the muzzle of his supposedly faithful hound.

To all appearances, the hound had attacked and killed the child. In anger and despair, the noble attacked the hound and killed it. Only then did he see that the infant was not dead and that below the crib lay a large and very dead snake (linked in Christian mythology to Satan himself). Rather than attacking the infant, the faithful hound had protected the crib and slain the creature that had tried to attack it. The nobleman was beside himself with grief and remorse. He buried the hound in a holy well around which he planted a grove of trees, as it was an ancient Celtic custom. Local people, hearing of the innocent dog's heroic act, made pilgrimages to the place and left stones there to form a shrine. Gradually, the fame of Guinefort grew, and spread to some other places in France. A text *De Adortione Guinefort Canis* (*Concerning the Dog Guinefort*) began to circulate, and the story is mentioned by the medieval writer Simon of Bourbon (d. 1262). A cult grew around the buried dog that rivaled any saint, naming the hound as the holy protector of small children. Indeed, there was a clamor for the creature to be fully made a saint. This is where the Church stepped in. It is forbidden under canon law to accord *any* animal saintly status, although it *can* be declared a heretic.

Nevertheless, a compromise was reached. The name *Guinefort* was attached to a Burgundian saint and the Church declared that the holy dog had actually been changed into a man. God, it decreed, had the power to grant a soul to an animal if it showed goodness and heroism, thus changing it into human form. But, it warned, He conversely also had the power to change men into beasts if they showed sinful or lewd behavior. Thus, Guinefort became known all across medieval France as "the dog saint," a holy man who was linked to a canine. The obverse of this was, of course, the werewolf—the man who changed into a canine. A nearly identical story to that of Guinefort comes from Wales, where St. Gelert was once said to be the favorite hound of Llewellyn the Great, a ruler of Gwennyd. He too was changed into a man.

A slightly similar story is sometimes also associated with St. Roche of Montpellier, who was served by a faithful and holy dog who stole bread from its master's table to take to the saint when he lay as a plague victim in the forest. In some stories, the animal was rewarded for this holy act by the gift of a soul, thus changing it into a man, similar to St. Guinefort. From then on, the dog-man drops from history and legend.

St. Christopher

But St. Guinefort and St. Roche are not the only holy men who have strong canine connections. The most famous was, of course, St. Christopher, the patron saint of travelers, who in certain medieval depictions of him boasts a dog's head. The name *Christopher* is usually taken to mean "Christ-bearer," but this version is a Greek variation of a baptismal name that was given to him. In Latin his original name is *Reprebus*, which is a corruption of the name *Reprobus*, meaning "wicked." According to ancient tradition, Christopher was one of a dog-headed race whose name is sometimes given as the Marmaritae (supposedly from an obscure country known as Marmarica somewhere in North Africa). It was also said that in his earlier life, Christopher was an eater of human flesh and spoke only in the harsh and guttural language of the dog-headed race.

On hearing the words of a Christian prophet, who preached on the borders of his country, Christopher began to meditate upon his condition and upon his own practices. As he did so an angel appeared and touched his mouth, so that he could speak in languages that all men would understand. At this Christopher left his own country and traveled into the Greek world where he began to proclaim the Christian Gospel to all who would listen—becoming a forceful missionary in a number of lands. This, according to some traditions, is what his name *really* meant, for he bore the word of Christ into many Pagan lands. However, he still remained a dog-headed figure, and the Church was still highly suspicious of him.

The story of Christopher as a dog-head persisted long into the medieval period, especially in Ireland where the monks of the Celtic Church still used Greek script (the story of Christopher was widely written in Greek) rather than Latin, and relayed the story among the many monasteries of the island. The venerable *Leabar Brac* (the *Speckled Book*) contains an eighth century Irish kalendar of saints, explicitly stating that Christopher was a member of a dog-headed race, he ate human flesh, and as he mediated on God, he could only speak the language of the dog-heads. A contemporary English writer, Walter of Speyer, also gives two biographies of the saint (one in prose and one in verse), which also allude to the fact that Chrisopher had a dog's head and that he came from a race of similar creatures.

The story may originate from the reign of Roman Emperor Diocletian (284–6 alone and 286–305 with Maximan). During this time, it is said that a certain warrior named Reprobus ("scoundrel") was captured in battle and brought to Rome as a prisoner. He was said to be bigger than any ordinary human, more muscular, and with the head of a dog. He came from Marmarica, which was either in North Africa or somewhere further east, and was said to boast prodigious strength. The story may have generated around a Berber warrior from the Atlas Mountains of modern-day Morocco, who, although not having the head of a dog, was certainly of more than average stature and a fierce fighter. The questionable attributes of this man were later transferred to the saint.

Christopher, of course, is always considered something of a problematic saint with strong Pagan connections. In other versions of the tale, he is fully human, but a giant—a member of an ancient race that once walked the earth. It is in this guise that he bears the Christ-child upon his shoulders across the raging torrent. In some instances, he was not really considered to be a saint, and thus equal to the other Fathers of the Church. Although his name had existed since the English Middle Ages, some even questioned if he had existed at all. Latterly, his name was "struck off" the list of official saints; though he may still be venerated in some quarters he is not officially recognized by the Vatican.

Dog-Headed Saints

Although Christopher is perhaps the best-known of the allegedly dog-headed saints, there may well have been others. There are references in some texts, for example, to an Eastern holy man—St. Andrew Cynocephali (the name is taken to mean "dog-headed") of Kokar Kilese, part of Cappadocia in modern-day Turkey. Nothing much is known of this saint, and it is possible that such a character results from an early Christian legend concerning St. Andrew and St. Bartholomew. In this tale, the two saints ventured among the Parthians (an influential people living on a central plateau in modern-day Iran). They found their cities "abominable" and the people practicing cannibalism. It is said that some of the high magistrates of their settlements boasted the heads of dogs—though this may have been more of a generalized term of abuse—and that Andrew in particular preached against them. It is possible that the story got confused with the references to a Turkish saint, attributing the dog's head to him.

The Dog-Headed Race

The idea of dog-headed saints, of course, also opens up the question of races of dog-headed people living somewhere in the world. As explorers traveled further and further across the medieval world, they returned with tales of the great wonders and strange people to be found in foreign lands. They spoke of men with a large eye in the center of their stomachs, of races with impossibly long ears, of beings who hopped only on one foot—every story a possible exaggeration, a misinterpretation, or a flight of imagination or hyperbole. One of the oldest of these legendary races were the dog-heads who had appeared in fables and stories since earliest times. The belief in a dog-headed race was incredibly widespread, especially in western Europe—after all, as we noted previously, St. Christopher was supposed to have come from that race. However, as to where such a race actually *lived,* the matter was open to speculation. In medieval Europe, their country was supposed to lie somewhere in the East, although its exact location was difficult to specify. Conversely, when contact was made with several Eastern realms it was found that they too had stories about the dog-heads, only in their case the species dwelt in the *west.* Northern Africa, inhabited by the Moors, was considered to be exotic, barbarous, and a suitable place for a cannibalistic dog-headed race, as were certain remote areas of Greece and Turkey. Few people had visited such areas, and the myth of the dog-heads living there was greatly strengthened by their remoteness and inaccessibility. Pliny, for instance, citing a Greek source, claimed that the creatures lived in the mountains of India, and this seemed to be borne out by some marvelous stories from that area concerning the conquests of Alexander the Great. Other areas, however, were also mentioned, such as Mesopotamia, Judea, remote parts of Egypt, Crete, and Arabia. They seemed to inhabit any area that was away from the known world, and which might appear threatening or dangerous to the traveler.

Some of these races of dog-heads were also alleged to dwell on remote islands. In the *Voiage de Sir John de Maundeville*, which appeared in 1357 and was supposedly a true account of the voyages of a 14th century explorer, there is a reference to a race known as the Carnophales, who dwell on the island of Necumera somewhere in the Western Ocean. These people had the heads of dogs, were much taller than any human being, and were extremely primitive. The exact location of their island was never specified, but their existence was certainly taken as an incontrovertible fact. Although called the Carnophales here, the most common name for such a species was Cynocephali (a term that was also used to describe St. Christopher), which usually referred to a dog-headed race living on one of the more distant isles of the Aegean. These were believed by the Greeks to be both monstrous and primitive, and they spoke in a barking voice—in fact, our word *barbarian* is taken from the Greek mockery of such a tongue, which they also equated with foreigners—"Bar bar" (which is similar to the childish "bow-wow" representing the barking of a dog).

If such beings *did* exist, the question was then asked as to what manner of creatures they were—were they men or beasts? Did they have souls or not? Could they attain salvation through Christ as did other men? The great thinkers and churchmen of the time hotly debated the issue. Some learned men argued that if the dog-heads existed, they were simply another branch of mankind. Others, however, argued that they were no more than ravening beasts and pointed to their alleged cannibalism and supposedly ferocious behavior. Foremost in the denunciation of the dog-headed race was the Church, which declared them as little more than "brute beasts." They would not enjoy Christ's salvation, the prelates declared, because they were not true men, had no souls, and were completely given over to animal lusts. A number of theologians, however, disagreed, citing John 10:16, which seemed to imply that there were other non-Christian peoples in the world that would benefit from Christ's

message. They argued that it was the Christian duty to bring the Gospels to the dog-headed peoples wherever they might be. One such thinker was the ninth-century Frankish monk Ratramnus, resident at the Corbie monastery (near Amiens) in Picardy who died around AD 868. Ratramnus was considered to be an unorthodox thinker and a colleague (and something of an intellectual opponent); Radbertus Paschasius, while considering the religious status of the dog-headed race, had asked him what he thought of them. The answer was given in the form of a letter; *Epsitola de Cynocephali* is a curious document. In it, Ratramus lays out his belief that the dog-heads are a "decayed" branch of the race of Adam (that is, another form of humanity), and, as such, may well be entitled to Eternal Salvation as any other. His views, of course, did not find favor with the Church or any intellectuals of his day, and his writing were later denounced as heresy by the Synod of Vercelli in 1050. He also questioned transubstantiation, declaring it to be merely "a symbol."

Undeterred by such thinking and writing, the Western Church continued to denounce the dog-heads as both Pagan and ungodly. They cited the Christian legend of the father of St. Mercurius who was torn to pieces by two Cynocephali and would also have attacked the saint had the saint not called upon St. Michael. (Some of the dog-heads were later converted to Christianity as a result of St. Mercurius's teachings and were rendered gentle, but the Church argued that this did not wholly take away from their innate bestial nature.) Such monstrous appearance and behavior, argued the Church Fathers, were the outward signs of the heresy of such races.

The Eastern Church, however, held a more ambiguous position. Relying on biblical accounts of the descent of the Holy Spirit upon the Disciples at Pentecost and their linguistic conversions when they preached (every man could hear in his own tongue), they asserted that every nation upon the face of the earth should receive the Gospel in its own language aided by the Holy Paraclete (Holy Ghost). This might have included the dog-headed races living in remote areas. Thus, the 11th-century *Theodore Psalter* (one of the most valuable illuminated manuscripts from the Byzantine Empire, now held in the British Library) depicts Christ preaching to dog-headed men who listen attentively. An Armenian Gospel dating from around AD 1262 also shows a similar scene: Christ bringing the word of God to a dog-headed nation. This is described as a combination of "Medes, Parthians, and Elamites," implicitly placing these people amongst the cynocephali. Other stories from Byzantium further mention missionaries going out into the lands where the "dog-heads" lived seeking to convert them, but there is no indication if such conversions (apart from Christopher) were ever successful.

Thus, the medieval view of the alleged dog-headed peoples was a confused one. On one hand, they were brute beasts who represented the forces of Pagan darkness and were probably agents of the Devil, while on the other hand they might be an off-shoot of mankind in need of the redemption that the Gospels offered. The idea that the dog-heads were implacable enemies of Christianity gained more credence during the Crusades and the wars against the Muslims in the Holy Land. Many Islamic rulers during this time became equated with dog-heads and the forces of darkness, seeking to subvert or overthrow the Christian message. Depictions of Arabic or Middle Eastern rulers usually showed them in splendid robes, but with dogs-heads. For example, a world map of 1430, which denotes a people known as the Beni Chelib, contains the legend "Ebinichebel is a Saracen Ethiopian king with his dog-headed people." Indeed, the name of the people comes from a Latin translation of the original Arabic phrase meaning "sons of a dog." This king was Ethiopian and his people were Muslim, and gradually the name *dog-head* or *dog people* was becoming a term of abuse or contempt, relating to "Saracens" throughout the medieval Christian world. It emphasises the "Paganness" of such people and their distance from correct (Christian) theology and practice. Such contempt was widened to include Jews, who were sometimes portrayed with the heads of dogs or foxes right up until the 16th century and beyond, suggesting slyness and maliciousness. The fact that the Jews had crucified Christ only added to the perceptions of devilry and bestiality, which the Christians attributed to them, and therefore placed them well within the monstrous realm of evil.

Ktesias

But it was not only the Muslim and Jewish people of the Middle East that were accorded canine attributes in the medieval mind. Further east, in the mountains of India, large numbers of dog-heads were also believed to dwell. The belief was based on the writing of Ktesias of Knidos, who lived at the end of the fourth century BC; he claimed that there were 120,000 dog-headed people living among the remote Indian mountains. Ktesais came from the Island of Kos in the Aegean and was reputedly one of the Asklepion School doctors. (The sanatorium at Asklepion—dedicated to Apollo—was one of the foremost medical academies in ancient Greece. One of its students was the great Hippocrates, now know as the "father of medicine.") Ktesias was appointed as a physician to the Persian king Artaxerxes II, and was granted access to a marvelous library filled with obscure books and texts that the monarch held. He was allowed to copy certain scrolls detailing Persian travels in many lands and of the wonders encountered there, which he later reproduced in a series of his own books.

In some of these he referred to a species of man known as the kyrokephaloi (cynocephali?) who dwelt in remote valleys in the mountains of India and who were many in number. They had the faces of dogs and only spoke in a harsh barking tongue or by expressions of the hands when they dealt with other races. The Persians found them exceptionally fierce and warlike with a great appetite for human flesh. These creatures were indeed cannibals and their culture was exceptionally primitive—they dressed in the hides of animals and lived in very rough dwellings and in caves. For the most part they were farmers, growing crops and tilling the land in the high mountains around the Upper Indus River, but they could also be extremely savage and ferocious if a stranger wandered into their areas—attacking him or her as a dog would. Ktesias advised that they were to be avoided.

Many subsequent writers questioned Ktesias's veracity. The writer Lucian heaped a great deal of scorn upon his writings, implying that he never had any access to such an archive (if it actually existed) and had simply made the details up or that they were based on rumors and gossip. And there seems to be some substance to these claims, for although Artaxerxes did possess a library, it may not have been nearly as extensive as Ktesias stated. There were, however, stories of dog-headed people living in the Indian mountains—indeed, reference had been made to a canine-looking people in accounts from the travels of Marco Polo and from some of the writings concerning the Eastern conquests of Alexander the Great. They were indeed described as cannibals and as being "primitive" in their culture. However, such accounts stopped short of describing them as being fully "dog-headed"—probably as sharp-faced and with rather protruding canine teeth. Nevertheless, Ktesias's account took hold on the Western medieval mind, and it was taken as a certainty that dog-headed races lay somewhere in the Far East.

Other Writings

This belief was strengthened by writers such as Thomas of Cantimpre (1201–1272), who published a work entitled *Liber de Monstruosis Hominibus Orientis* (*Book of the Monstrous Men of the Orient*) to great acclaim in the 13th century. Also writing around the same time was Giovanni de Pian dei Carine (1180–1252), one of the first Europeans to visit the court of the great Eastern Khans, who recorded how the forces of the Ogedei Khan (Genghis Kahn's third son, 1186–1241) had encountered and fought with a race of dog-headed men near the Dalai-Nor (the Northern Sea—now identified as Lake Baikab in Southern Siberia). These men fought exceptionally well and were reputed to be cannibals.

Writing in the *Speculum Naturalis* for his patron, King Louis IX of France, the venerable encyclopedist, Vincent of Beauvais (c1190–1264) describes what he believes to be a man-wolf from the East. He is, says Vincent, "an animal with the head of a dog but with all other members of human appearance. Though he behaves like a man…and when peaceful, he is tender like a man; when furious, he becomes cruel and retaliates against humankind." His image reflected a number of other medieval writers including the mysterious Adam of Bremen, thought to have been born around 1050, and whose template of the man-wolf would spawn many imitators among the courtly scribes.

Maps

The idea of dog-headed people, living in some wild place far outside the Christian sphere of influence was beginning to take a deep root in the Western medieval mind. In fact, on many medieval maps, the *Terra Incognita* (unknown lands) were often characterized by pictures of such creatures. They represented all that was alien and mysterious about these distant places—and perhaps what was dangerous as well. Dog-heads appeared on many medieval mappa mundae ("map of the world") denoting largely unexplored areas of the earth. They appear for example on the T and O map, which shows the earth as flat and only includes known habitable portions in Hereford Cathedral that dates from around 1079 to show unexplored lands where such beings were thought to exist. Such maps were based on ancient Greek and Roman maps, and they sometimes displayed lands that lay even beyond Greek or Latin knowledge and influence. These were counted as savage places where civilization had not really touched and that were inhabited only by barbarians, cannibals, and monsters. Many of these representations were simply people and creatures from classical myth and fable, some of which were adapted to wear the heads of dogs in order to demonstrate their ferocity and evil.

One such place was the land of the Laestrygonians with its capital Telephylos. This region had appeared in Homer's *Odyssey* as a place where the Ithacan king had landed and was captured by the inhabitants. These had been cannibalistic giants, and Odysseus and his men had been lucky to escape their clutches. Their home, referred to as "the rocky stronghold of Lamos" was often credited as a small island far beyond Sicily and therefore well away from the centers of civilization where primitive, violent creatures might dwell. (They pelted Odysseus's ships with rocks from the headlands above.) Some of the Laestrygonians are portrayed in later maps as having the heads of dogs, although there is no reference to this in Homer's original tale.

A number of these fantastic tales may have resulted from the man-like animals that travelers sometimes witnessed in these far-away locations—gorillas, sharp-faced monkeys, baboons, and mandrills. These were then transformed into fantastic people, who were probably both ferocious and dangerous. As the medieval period continued, the list of writers who included such beings (or stories about them) began to grow, attributing greater ferocity, greater wickedness, and sometimes greater supernatural powers to them. The motif of the savage, dog-headed, man-shaped predator was already starting to emerge in the Western imagination during this period.

Chinese Legend

In eastern areas such as China, the idea of the dog-headed being was a little different and was tied up with the creation myth. In the distant past, according to legend, the earth was devastated by a great flood that destroyed all life. Only the Chinese god-hero Fu Hsi and his wife were spared. They avoided the rising water by fleeing to the top of Mount Kunlun in central China from where, realizing that they were the only people left, they implored the Emperor of the Heavens to give them some company. This the Celestial Being did by granting Fu Hsi the power to make living people from the soft clay that had been left after the Flood. He created figures that he baked in the hot sun, which then sprang to life at his command. Some of his first creations were not very good, particularly those that had faces resembling dogs, which the creator had mistakenly given them. These creations also came to life, but were driven away into "the far mountains" or into "a far land beyond the sea" where they continued to live, well away from the proper creations that the god-hero (and later ruler of his people) had correctly fashioned. What actually became of them is never revealed.

A further mention of dog-headed people is made in an extremely ancient Chinese work known as the *Liang Shu* (*A History of the Liang Dynasty*), which is of uncertain age and authorship. This mentions a race of Cynocephali dwelling on an island to the east of the country of Fusang. In Chinese legend, Fusang was not wholly regarded as an actual country, but as a place that lay far away to the West. In fact, some scholars have identified this idealized location as America. Others suggest it may have been Japan, although the Chinese often referred to this land simply as Wo. It was a land that first came to the attentions of the Chinese through the writings of the 17th-century Buddhist missionary Han Shan, who claimed to have landed there, although his descriptions of it are often confused. Wherever it was, fierce and rather primitive dog-headed people dwelt there in profusion, frequently attacking those Chinese explorers and traders who dared to land upon their shores.

As in the West, the Eastern view of the dog-heads was somewhat mixed. Some tended to view them as a civilized people who were an offshoot of humanity itself, created by Fu Hsi, others as fierce and war-like beings who usually attacked those who came to visit them. Just as in Europe, the distinction between the civilized man and the ravening beast—the basis for our common image of the werewolf—was becoming apparent even in the East.

Japan

But it was not only various distant races of such animalistic peoples that exercised the Eastern mind. Individuals closer to home could also display the characteristics of canines—or more specifically, foxes. In both China and Japan certain people living in certain—usually rural—communities, were believed to exhibit fox-like characteristics and traits. This is because they actually *were* foxes, who by some supernatural means, had acquired human shape. Such persons were usually regarded ambiguously by those around them. In many Eastern cultures, foxes are not regarded as being completely evil, although they are sometimes regarded as tricky creatures. But they are also considered to be wise, and in some places they are even venerated; there are fox shrines in many locations across Japan in order to facilitate such worship. The Japanese word for fox—*kitsuni*—usually became synonymous with the word *yokai*, which often meant a capricious spirit, giving it an even greater mystical interpretation as a *fox spirit.* So those who demonstrated their characteristics—the were-foxes—were often considered to have special powers or a special wisdom, but they could also be extremely tricky, have a connection to fickle spirits, and should not be crossed. They could, it was believed, revert to their true fox form whenever they chose, but it was an effort for them to retain their human shape, so some transformations occurred spontaneously when they had a momentary lapse. If, for example, they became drunk, they would completely lose their shape and might even return to the wild for a time. Also some of the changes that they made into human shapes were incomplete. In some stories both men and women (though in many were-fox stories, the fox tends to take on a female shape) strove to hide a fox's tail under their clothes in order to avoid detection by their neighbors or friends. Such people were also believed to have incredible magical powers, and it was thought that many local witches were foxes in disguise.

For the sake of understanding and explaining the concept, the Japanese sometimes divided their fox-people into two distinct categories—the *zenke,* or good foxes, and the *yako,* literally "outsider foxes," those who were mischievous or who might cause harm. This rule of thumb was not completely absolute, but served as a rough guide to the creature's often ambivalent nature. The *zenko* were said to be worshipped as fox spirits and the *yako* were to be generally avoided. Thus, the notion of duality in the canine form—either beneficent (cultured) or ferocious (barbaric) began to be fixed throughout the various cultures—even those of the Far East.

The classic ideal of the werewolf—the civilized man who can be turned into the feral beast—gradually emerged out of this basic concept. Other elements—cannibalism, devil worship, and so on—were added on later, but the dichotomy between civilization and savagery would underpin them all. There were, however, other elements that grew out of such a basic notion too—the notion of the shapeshifter or of the warrior who could change his appearance in battle—and it is to this belief system that we now turn. Here, the wolf cast a very long shadow.

2

Man Into Beast

When thou, as a wolf,
Wanderest in the woods,
Knowing no fortune,
Nor any pleasure.

—Helgakvioa Hundingsbana, Second Edition

Some of the things that early men admired about the wild beasts they encountered in the forests and the plains were strength, ferocity, and extreme cunning, not only in the hunt, but also when they fought with other creatures. They wished that they could have such attributes too—particularly when they faced their enemies. And, of course, in the early years of civilization when the distinction between men and beasts may have been blurred—especially in western Europe and the northern climes.

Transformation Beginnings

The early shamans, as has already been noted, believed that by donning the skin of the animal—be it a wolf or some other creature—or by adopting the mannerisms of the beast, hunters and warriors could gain some of these attributes for themselves. These pelts would then supernaturally develop into a "second skin," transforming the wearer into the animal concerned.

According the late historian and folklorist Reverend Sabine Baring-Gold, there was a group of men known as the *eigi einhamr* (meaning "not of one skin") in Norway and Iceland. It was widely believed that these men could take on any appearance that they chose, whether human or animal, as well as the nature of the specific person or creature. The new shape was called *hamr*, which, confusingly, was also a name often used to describe the original form. The actual process of transformation was known as *skipta homum* or sometimes *at hamas*. If such people took on the guise of a wild animal, their strength and cunning would increase, and they might acquire other extraordinary powers, such as hearing or smell. This transformation was a deliberate one on the part of the individual concerned, and was brought about in various supernatural ways. For instance, the skin of an animal would be thrown over the body whose essence (or soul) would then take on the form of the creature, leaving the human form limp and inert, as if it were dead. Other methods used were the incantation of certain spells or the application of ointments or unguents. In this case, the original form of the person remained unaltered, but the *perception* of him or her in the eyes of the beholders changed the appearance, which he or she had selected, and he or she would adopt the characteristics of the creature. The only way to know that the animal was *eigi einhamr* was by looking directly at its eyes, which no magic could alter. It was generally thought that many Nordic shamans and black magicians took on such guises, often for various malefic purposes.

Dark Secrets

The donning of skins, both human and animal, was not unknown in northern folklore although it was invariably associated with darkest sorcery. The famous nabrock trousers or "corpse breeches" were often a staple of Icelandic tales concerning witches and warlocks. These ghastly items of clothing comprised the feet, legs, and lower body (including the genitals) cut from a newly interred corpse and fashioned into a pair of trousers or breeches. These were then worn by the black magician after certain incantations had been said. Sometime during the hours of darkness, the magicians would fill them up with gold (particularly the scrotum if the corpse had been male). The trousers were also said to give the wearer certain supernatural powers and were the stock in trade of many Icelandic sorcerers.

It was said that the "most evil man in Iceland," Gottskalk Grimmi Nikulasson (Gottskalk the Grim, Bishop of Holar 1496–1520—one of the last Catholic Bishops in Iceland), author of the celebrated *Raudskinna* (the *Red Skinned Grimoire*), left detailed instructions on how to create the nabrock trousers, as well as skin cloaks for turning men into the semblance of animals.

Such secrets were also taught at the famous Black Schools of Iceland—these were schools of dark magic hidden away in secret locations, scattered across the countryside. These schools spawned some of the most evil magicians in the Nordic lands. Although shape-changing did not feature all that heavily in the witchcraft trials that gripped Iceland between 1625 and 1683, in which more than 21 people were burned, local stories did feature people who could change themselves into the guise of ferocious animals and threaten their neighbors.

Shape Changers

In the *Landnamabok* (a 9th- or 10th-century manuscript known as *The Book of Settlement* detailing early settlement in Iceland) there is an account of an ancient man who saw in a dream two animals fighting over the division of land. These he recognized as two of his neighbors who were supposedly *eigi einhamr*. One of these combatants was a Finn—the Icelanders believed that the Finns as a race were great magicians and could take on animal forms whenever they chose.

The Nordic gods and goddesses too often took on the forms of animals using special clothing for the purpose. Frigg and Freya, for instance, used *valshmr* or "falcon mantles," cloaks made from the feathers of falcons, to travel about the land in the guise of birds. This cloak was also used by Loki, the god of mischief, to carry out pranks on unsuspecting humans for his own amusement. But the greatest and most coveted article of such clothing was the *ulfahamr*, or wolf shirt, which gave the wearer all the qualities a warrior admired—courage, ferocity, strength, and cunning. These were all the qualities that the wolf possessed and that mankind yearned for. These qualities were also extended to the bear—a common creature in early northern climes—and in many ways the bear pelt became steeped in folklore and as sought after as the wolf. Indeed, it was believed that if a warrior wore the skin of a bear, he would also acquire certain desired attributes of the wolf: great strength, ferociousness, and combative prowess.

Norse legend speaks of a group of soldiers, followers of the god Odin, among the troops of certain Viking kings, who were known as "berserkers," from the Danish "bar-sark," which is said to mean "bear shirt" (although the exact etymology of the word has been hotly disputed by some scholars). It is from these fighters that the term *berserk,* meaning mad or uncontrollable, has crept into the English language. These were elite warriors, clad in either wolfskins or bearskins who fought on behalf of the god, but who attached themselves to the armies of Norse kings known for their ferocity and bloodlust in battle. Prior to any fight, they whipped themselves into a frenzy or trance, during which all reason seemed to leave them and they became almost uncontrollable, taking on aspects of the animal whose pelts they wore. They fought without bodily armor or protection, and this has caused some historians to suggest that the berserkers fought "bare (rather than bear) skinned" (that is, without the benefit of chain mail). However, in Scandinavian literature they are referred to as "Ulfheohar" or "men dressed in wolfskins"—a symbol of their connection to the animal. They were both worshipped and feared, and much sought-after by ancient Norse rulers because of their ferocity.

Berserkers

The earliest reference to the berserkers appears in a 9th-century Norse poetic work known as the *Haraldskaeoi*—a skaldic verse written by Thorbjorn Hornklofi in praise of King Harald Fairhair of Norway (AD c. 870–930). The skalds were often poets at the court of a Scandinavian king who wrote great eulogies concerning their rulers in a form of meter known as malahattr. It was said that the berserkers served as part of Harald's army in a number of campaigns, and that they were regarded as fearsome fighters. In the saga they were said to be the followers of the Norse wargod Tyr (although later accounts describe them as followers of Odin, the supreme Norse god), and state that they fought for Harald at the Battle of Hafrafjord against a confederation of Danes and others, where they achieved great slaughter. The account, preserved by the Norse poet Snorri Sturlson (1179–1241), has long been open to controversy about its accuracy, as has the role played by the so-called berserkers. Some argue that they may have been an exaggeration created by Snorri himself.

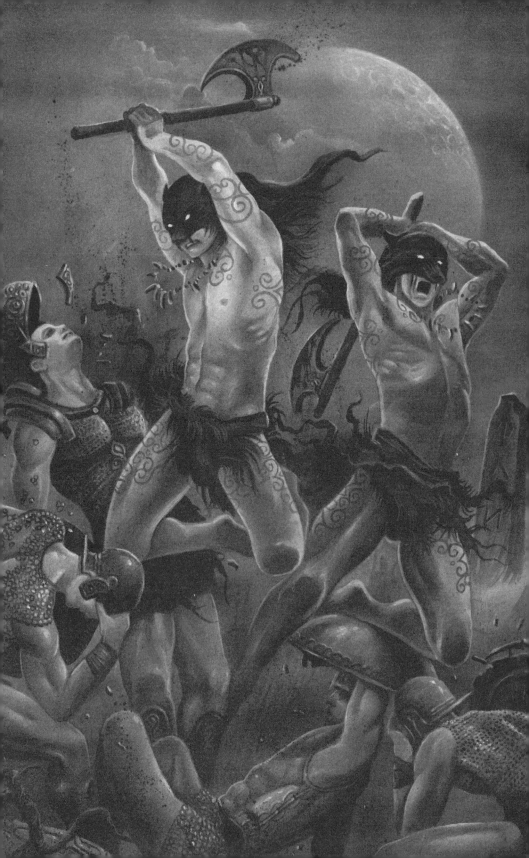

Berserkers also appear in the *Saga of Hrolf Kraki* (also known as *Rolf Krenge*). Kraki was a legendary Danish king who also appears in some Anglo-Norse accounts and folktales from eastern England where the Danes once held power. Here, the berserkers are described simply as a band of outlaws dressed in wolf and bear pelts, who rampage through various neighborhoods, plundering, burning, and pillaging. In the ancient 13th-century Icelandic work *Njal's Saga* (also known as *The Burning of Njal*—one of the oldest complete Icelandic texts), a captured berserker is used to test two fires—one lit by the Pagans and the other by the Christians. The fire of the Christian completely consumes the Pagan outlaw, thus proving the strength and dominance of the religion.

The most famous berserker, however, was the Icelandic farmer and warrior Egill Skallagrimson, who has become one of the great villains/anti-heroes of Icelandic literature. His exploits are recorded in *Egills Saga*, again adapted and written by the poet Snorri Sturlson, which was at one time considered to be a classic of Northern literature. Egill came from a long line of dubious persons—his grandfather Ulf was also known as Kveldulfr, which means "Evening Wolf," and was considered to be a notorious magician and shapeshifter, taking on the form of a wolf when he chose. His father, Skella-Grimr Kveldulfrson, was also a feared berserker and was credited with killing many men when in fits of uncontrollable rage. As a berserker Egill seemed to have a number of supernatural powers, including the gift of healing—in fact, he apparently performed a number of healing miracles. He was also a great poet in the skaldic tradition, allegedly writing his first verse at a very early age. As a warrior, he is said to have fought for Harald Fairhair, the Norwegian king, as part of the latter's "shock troops," as he consolidated Norway under a single ruler and drove out Danish settlers. It is said that Egill alternately wore the pelt of a wolf and the pelt of a bear, and he describes fighting with men and tearing out their jugular veins with his bare teeth. There is no doubt that he was greatly feared.

Despite Harald Fairhair's use of them in his army, the use of berserkers among Viking troops sometimes presented a problem—especially when it came to discipline. Several old Irish accounts of the Battle of Clontarf near Dublin in 1014 (a conflict in which Viking Ireland took on its Celtic counterpart under the Irish king Brian Boru) speak of berserkers rioting through both Irish and Viking villages, creating great destruction to their own side as well as to the Irish. And there were problems at home in Norway too, as troops of berserkers attacked their own villages upon returning home from war (the "battle-rage" was still in them). In 1015, the Norwegian Jarl (local ruler) Hakenarson, forbade berserkers anywhere in the area of the country; he ordered them to be hunted down and executed. By the early 1100s the organized berserker bands that characterized some of the armies of the Scandinavian kings had all but disappeared.

Nature of the Beast

What caused the "berserking fury"—the bloodshot eyes and the raging nature—in many of these men? For many of their contemporaries, the answer was a supernatural one—they were simply "possessed" by a totemic animal spirit. Such "possession" was usually a voluntary one, with the spirit being summoned by special incantations and invited to inhabit the body of the warrior. As soon as it had done so, the person's demeanor (and often his physical appearance) seemed to change. His eyes became glazed or bloodshot, his hair extended as if by electric shock, he might have grown in stature, and his strength and ferocity increased. Such "possession" was often aided by the wearing of the skin or pelt—usually wolf or bear—of the animal concerned and by adopting mannerisms consistent with the creature whose spirit was sought. Recently, however, some scientists have suggested that there may have been some form of external chemical cause for the berserker nature. They state that an infusion of bog myrtle—a plant used in the preparation of a number of Scandinavian alcoholic beverages—may have been used to induce the berserker state. This infusion may have been a part of the "spirit summoning" ritual. Scientists also point to a number of mushrooms in the region that have psychoactive properties and might have produced such an effect.

In 1784, the Swedish botanist Samuel Odman drew attention to the agaric mushroom (*amanita muscaria*), which, although toxic when taken in large quantities, also has hallucogenic qualities when ingested in small amounts. This mushroom was actually used as part of shamanistic ritual in Eastern Siberia, and it is possible that it was used in ancient Scandinavian religion as well—probably to induce a berserker state among warriors. However, recent tests (2004/2005) show that the use of such fungus-based drugs actually *slows* reaction time and the ability to use ancient Viking weapons, and it was therefore suggested that the berserker state was probably achieved by some psychological means, although no specific arousal technique has so far been identified. The concept of the berserker remains an enigma, but there can be no doubt that it laid the foundations for the idea of the modern-day werewolf.

Nor were the Norse the only people to exhibit the "killing frenzy" in which animalistic behavior and/or mannerisms came to the fore. Stories appear in the *Iliad* that tell of Greek warriors who could send themselves into "frenzies" at will. This was reputedly particularly common among the Spartans, and there is mention of a certain Aristodemus, who was involved in a killing frenzy in which he seemed to physically change during the Battle of Platoea in Boetia (north of the Gulf of Corinth) against the Persians in 479 BC.

Irish Beasts

Ancient Irish heroes were also capable of bringing on such animalistic behavior and changing their appearance into a frightening guise in order to terrify their enemies. The most famous of these was Cu-Cuhullain—the "Cu" in front of his name signifying "hound" or "dog"—who also became "possessed" in the heat of battle. But many other warriors were also capable of the "battle fury" during conflicts between the various Irish kings. Many of these were believed to be the result of a dog or spirit temporarily taking over their bodies. In most cases, the fury passed when they were doused with cold water.

There also seem to be groups of "wolf-men" (akin to berserkers) in Irish literature too. An extremely ancient manuscript, the *Coir Anmann* (edited in the 16th century) speaks of a group of warriors in old Ireland who were known as the Laignech Faelad; they fought alongside some of the ancient kings, who were famed for their ferocity. They may well have been berserkers, although the *Coir* states that they could actually alter their shape to ravening wolves whenever they so chose. In return for their prowess in battle they demanded no payment—only human flesh, particularly that of very young infants, which they consumed with alarming and despicable gusto.

Writing slightly later than the editing of the ancient text, the English historian William Camden spoke mockingly of "The Wolf Men of Tipperary," whom he said might have been the last remnants of these ancient warriors. Stories about them, sneered Camden, may have been no more than the imaginations of an extremely credulous people. Despite Camden's skepticism, however, belief in the existence of the ancient Laignech Faelad continued in Ireland and more and more gruesome detail was added to their name. They were the followers of the Crom Cruach—Bowed Crom of the Mounds—one of Ireland's oldest and bloodiest gods; they practiced human sacrifice and they could take on the form of wolves when they pleased. When in battle, they howled like wild beasts, and when they were not fighting, they dwelt in remote places away from human habitation. Whether or not these beings actually existed, the idea of the wolf-man, dwelling alone perhaps in the forest and possibly exhibiting cannibalistic tendencies, was starting to take shape.

Although by the 12th century, many of the berserker groupings of northern and western Europe had more or less been disbanded and had ceased to exist, the memory of them lingered on, and became almost a byword for savage and unacceptable behavior. As many societies settled down and became much more stable, the idea of the "wild man," given to ungovernable rages, was pushed more and more to the periphery. Animalistic behavior was no longer to be tolerated. The wolf—or the man dressed in wolf's pelt—now became a social outcast and an outlaw.

Outlaws

One of the first real codifiers of a strict and generally recognizable legalized system in England were the Vikings, who, from around AD 800 until the mid-900s, occupied the eastern side of country in an area that became known as Danelaw or Danelagh. Although it formally collapsed around 950, elements of Danelaw and its kings remained until the 11th century. Danelaw also referred to a system of legal codes that had been hammered out between the Saxon King Alfred (847–899) and the Viking ruler Guthrum the Old (d. 890). This was an attempt to codify the "folk-rights," which had existed in certain parts of England (both Saxon and Viking), and a fraction of it dealt specifically with those who were on the fringes of society. Those who rose up against the common peace—murdering, pillaging, and looting—were to be treated like wild animals, hunted down, and killed. And the animal with which they were most identified was the wolf. The new codes used an old Latin phrase that had apparently existed since Roman times—*Caput great lupinum* (Let him be a wolf's head)—to identify criminals and disturbers of the peace. Perhaps it was some recollection of the berserkers that guided the Viking lawmakers to identify the wolf as the great enemy of humanity (although the Romans also may have similarly identified the animal), but the specter of the beast loomed large in the common imagination as both a savage miscreant and ravager. The term *wolf's head* became a byword for outlawry and pillage throughout the early English world. It was actually embodied as a legal term in the laws of King Cnut (or Canute), who formalized the laws of his predecessors. Under Cnut's laws, these "peripheral men" could be sought out, hunted down, and killed like wolves and have whatever property they possessed confiscated, without enjoying any form of legal protection. They were put "outside the peace" and defined as the foes of law-abiding men—it was clearly the actual duty of any community to destroy them as the vermin they were—they had become the wolf's head.

The behavior of such individuals only added to their animalistic perceptions. Living as they did, on the very periphery of organized society, such men existed by hunting animals in the wild woods and forests. As English society became better organized and the laws more regulatory, such areas often fell under the authority and control of local nobles, and the monarch and the animals that lived there became their property. The wild men who lived in the woods were pushed farther and farther to the edges of perceived society, becoming little more than wild animals themselves.

Man Into Beast

The first Norman ruler of England, William I (William the Conqueror 1066—1087), annexed great swathes of forest and turned them into Royal Parks to facilitate his own love of hunting. The deer and other animals that dwelt there became the king's own private property, and stringent laws were placed on any who hunted them or killed them for their own use—this, of course, included the wild men of the woodlands. An unnamed 11th-century monk records some of the laws that were brought in against those who dwelt in the Greenwood—the "forest men" or "wolf's heads":

> *Whoever slew a hart or hind,*
> *Was to be blinded*
> *He forbade the killing of boars,*
> *Even the killing of harts*
> *For he loved stags as dearly*
> *As though he was their own father.*

The laws did not, of course, stop or even limit the hunting of game in the forests, but it did further stigmatize those who hunted for food. Anyone who killed animals on the Royal Parks was now counted under law as a brute beast and subject to severe penalties, which were more appropriate to animals. Gradually, the general perception of such individuals began to change—if they were to be equated with beasts, then they *were* beasts. They were "wilde wolves" and seemed to have little to do with human society. They had chosen to live deep in the forests, away from civilized people, and their behavior often suggested that of the beast.

In the winter of 1279, a group of men, commonly regarded as outlaws and "wild men," emerged from the forest and attacked the village of Roxton in Bedfordshire, England, with an alarming savagery. Entering the village, they attacked the house of Ralph Bouveton, smashing down the walls with axes, creating mayhem and destruction, and killing all within. They then proceeded to the house next door where they slaughtered several others before proceeding to the house of John Cobbler, killing him and two of his daughters. The reason for such an attack is unclear, but it seems to have been motivated by hunger and a need to obtain food. The attack occurred in the wintertime when game was scarce and the wild men competed with other animals for sustenance.

A similar incident took place in the hamlet of Shipton in Oxfordshire in 1284 when a band of starving "forest men" attacked a mill and helped themselves to grain, and killed two women and a child in the process. Other such occurrences happened in rural parts of Herefordshire, Lincolnshire, and Yorkshire, and usually coincided with harsh winter months.

In parts of Europe, groups of "hedge soldiers" under localized commanders plundered, robbed, murdered, and lived in the wild. Outlaw bands such as these led by the psychopathic Bernard Garland in 14th-century France plagued villages and isolated castles continually while German "wild men," some resembling the berserkers of Norwegian lore, plundered and rampaged through parts of Saxony and Bavaria as late as the 15th century. Most of these men were desperate creatures often driven by poverty or hunger. The general impression of Robin Hood and his Merry Men living a civilized, quasi-idyllic existence in the Greenwood is, of course, no more than a romantic fantasy. Life for these "peripheral men" in the forests and mountains was invariably hard and demanding, and such a harsh existence usually brutalized the individuals concerned, making them little better than the animals with whom they shared their existence. They became as wolves, and the description "wolf's head" was often quite rightly applied to them, as they usually exhibited at least some of the traits of such canine predators. In some respects they were the archetypal "man-wolf," and this is how they were viewed by local communities—as "wolf-men."

The idea of feral men living on the very edge of society did not die out with the end of the medieval period, but continued as late as the 19th century. During the American Civil War (1861–1865) for example, groups of such men prowled remote areas, living rough and attacking isolated communities. These men were not really formal soldiers (although many styled themselves as such and proclaimed either the Union or Confederate cause), but rather "outlaws" who descended on remote farms and settlements without warning and taking what they wanted. Some defined themselves as "guerrillas" or "bushwhackers," and often attached themselves to loose bands of independent soldiery, such as the Kansas Redlegs, Missouri's Buttermilk Rangers, or groups led by William Clark Quantrill. Others, however, preferred to remain in the wild, such as the group led by Eli Wycher that terrorized parts of the Cumberland Plateau in Tennessee through the early days of the war. In some (admittedly questionable) accounts Wycher was slain like a wolf by the celebrated Tennessee Confederate guerrilla Champ Ferguson. These men, however, might be truly described as "feral," but followed in the tradition that had been established in early times.

Wodewose

Another early name that was also sometimes given to such individuals in England and parts of Europe was that of "woodwose" or "wodewose." The name is ambiguous, as it can alternately refer to a group of men or outlaws living in the forest, or to a mythical creature that existed deep in the woodlands since early times. This beast was described as being humanoid, big, and hairy, and the epitome of what we might imagine as the Himalayan Yeti or American

Sasquatch. This was a creature that was somewhere between a man and an animal. There is much evidence to suggest that the figure of the man-animal had a long history stretching back in Europe as far as classical times. Scholars have argued that the idea of the man-animal derives from the image in Enkidu, the beast-man, who appears in the Sumerian *Epic of Gilgamesh.* Enkidu acts and behaves like a beast—he is even covered in shaggy hair—because he has been raised by animals, and it is only by contact with civilization that the "wildness" leaves him and he becomes Gilgamish's champion. Later, the description of the woodwose became connected in the Hebrew mind with the Babylonian king Nebuchadnezzar II, who temporarily went mad and lived in the wild for seven years, eating grass, twigs, and raw meat, and attacking anyone who came close to him—the archetypal "wild man." (It has been argued by some medical historians that the monarch may have been suffering from a form of clinical boanthropy—a psychological disease in which suffers take the belief that they are in fact cattle.) However, the Hebrews believed that God had punished Nebuchadnezzar for his arrogance and vanity, and had made him "like a beast of the field." Alternatively, in England, it was associated with the wizard Merlin Wold, who, according to Geoffrey of Monmouth's *Vitae Merlin*, had gone mad for a time following the deaths of his brothers in battle. Apparently he had taken to living in the wild and subsisting on grass and herbs.

Other Sightings

A creature very much akin to the woodwose appears in some ancient Fankish (French) and German legends, where it is identified with local gods—possibly fertility deities. Indeed, it is a localized embodiment of nature and appears under a variety of local names—Orus, Pela, and Maia among others.

Reference to these names appears in an old ninth-century Spanish penitential, which describes their rites as being the remnants of ancient Pagan religions that were carried out in the worship of animalistic forest deities. There are other references, and in nearly every case, the being was supposed to be very wise—it had the cumulated wisdom of nature—but was also very ferocious and violent when crossed. There is also some evidence too that the Romans knew of a creature of the forest as Selinius—a very ancient, hairy, man-like entity who kept to the deep woods. According to the Greek historian Herodotus (489–435 BC), the creature inhabited the forests of an area that the Romans knew as Upper Dacia (between the Carpathian Mountains and the Danube River—currently encompassing Romania, Moldavia, and parts of Hungary), and was very rarely seen. Physically it was somewhere between man and beast—with the instincts of the human, but the temperament of an animal. Some writers even suggested that from time to time it had sexual congress with human women, and that offspring were produced, which invariably returned to the forest. In this respect it was the perfect fusion of man and animal.

For the Greeks, the forest-men were the embodiments (or servants) of the gods—linked in some way to the supernatural. The Greeks portrayed such creatures as the followers of Dionysus, the god of wine and hedonistic pleasures. They began to characterize them as having cloven feet—a sure mark of their animal nature—and this was later believed by the Christian Church in order to connect them with the Devil. The Romans described them as satyrs (Greek fauns)—half-human, half-goat, which combined the ideas of both human and beast; this strange coupling was reflected in their nature. On the one hand they were urbane and civilized (the human element), and on the other, they were capricious, tricky, and often sexually driven (the bestial side). They dwelt deep in the forests—into which they tried to lure humans—and were to be avoided by normal humans at all costs.

As both Greeks and Romans ventured farther across the world, they became aware of even more man-like animals. Some explorers such as the Carthaginian, Hanno the Navigator (late fifth-century BC), sailed as far as the coasts of Africa, where he found other beast men living in the forests close to the coast. These he named "gorillae" (from a Roman word meaning "a tribe of hairy women"), which has given us our modern word *gorilla*. Although we now know that this is a type of ape natural to the country, it was believed at the time to be an undiscovered type of creature that combined both the attributes of a man and an animal.

In England, the notion of the woodwose or animal-man continued as an embodiment of savage nature until the 16th or 17th centuries, and appears in a number of literary works including Edmund Spenser's *Faerie Queen*. It was supposed to dwell in places such as East Anglia, in parts of Norfolk, and Suffolk, where forests still proliferated. The creature remained a being of dual nature, cultured and civilized on one hand, and violent, depraved, and aggressive on the other. It was the clear delineation between civilized and savage, which would surface again in the werewolf motif.

Witchcraft

If certain entities could combine elements of both savagery and civilization, was it possible to shift between the two natures—for a civilized person to take on the very *guise* of an animal in the style of the *eigi einhamr*, as mentioned earlier? This was a question that taxed the minds of many thinkers and churchmen. Medieval Christian thought in the West seemed to suggest that it was, but only by using questionable supernatural powers. Such powers, argued the Church, could only come from the Devil, and so it was only those who had made a pact with the Infernal Master who could achieve such a change. These might include old women who had sold their souls to Satan in exchange for powers of transformation so they could perform acts of wickedness against their neighbors. Therefore, witches went about the countryside in the guise of cats, rats, stoats, and weasels, and even sometimes in the form of birds (crows and owls) or insects (beetles and cockroaches) in order to spy on those who lived near them or to carry out some evil deed. They usually accomplished such transformations either through the use of spells—ancient Saxon witchcraft supposedly used *galdor* or the configuration of certain runes—or by smearing their bodies with special ointments or unguents, the recipes for which they had obtained from various infernal sources. They might also cause such change through the wearing of a special piece of clothing that had "magical properties": a shirt, a dress, or a belt. As the Middle Ages reached their apogee, such beliefs became widespread across both England and Europe. In his *History and Topography of Ireland* written in 1187, the Welsh monk Gerald of Wales confidently asserted that all Irish women had the capacity to change themselves into hares and stoats at will. Gerald was, of course, incredibly gullible, and tended to believe everything that he was told, but the belief became incredibly widespread throughout Britain and continued until the mid-17th century.

A common folktale of the early 17th-century English countryside ran thus: "In Trent there was living at one time a girl who had inherited a witch's thong from her grandmother. When she tied this thong about herself, she would take on the likeness of a hare. In this form she heckled every forester that lived in the forests round about. When one of these men would shoot at her, his bolt glanced off her pelt." Writing in a similar vein, the English essayist and playwright John Marston (c. 1575–1634) describes "A hag whose lies shoot poisons that has become an ould witch and is now turning into a glib-cat." (A glib cat was a male cat that had been neutered.)

In Germany in 1427, a woman confessed that she had killed at least 30 infants by drinking their blood while in the guise of a cat. Curiously, she seemed to retain her human guise to everybody else, but appeared as a cat in her own eyes. In this guise, she claimed, she bit the infants as they lay asleep, drawing blood until they died. She made the confession to Bernardino of Sienna, who, with some satisfaction, arranged for her to be burned for her "crimes against Christianity."

The celebrated Scottish witch, Isobel Gowdie, the Witch of Auldearne near Nairn, was tried for sorcery in 1662 and admitted that she had from time to time taken on the guise of a cat in order to fulfil her enchantments throughout the countryside. She had affected the transformation from human to animal by reciting the following spell three times.

I shall goe intill aine catt,
With sorrow aine such and a blak shott,
An' I shall goe in the Divill's naim,
Aye, an' will I come again

In order to regain her human form, she claimed that the following counter charm had to be repeated three times:

Catt, Catt, God send thee blak shott,
I am in a catt's likeness just nao,
But I sal be in a woman's likeness ewen nao,
Catt, Catt, God send thee blak shott

In some versions of the story, she turned into a hare, in which case the rhyming couplet of the spell changed slightly, but the underlying process of transformation stayed the same.

Witch-hunts

In an official 1484 manual on witchcraft commissioned by Pope Innocent VIII, entitled *Malleus Malificarum* (*The Hammer of the Witch*), two Dominican Inquisitors—Jacobus Sprenger and Heinrich Kramer—detail how witches in parts of Germany can transform themselves into beasts simply by using spells, relics, or potions. This witch-hunter's handbook became the official position of the Catholic Church: some people under direction from the

Devil could change themselves into the guise of animals at will. The godly were exhorted to look out for and to denounce their wicked neighbors, who most assuredly could take on the form of an animal (even of a wolf) to attack those who went about God's work. The volume became widely read and was reprinted in various versions across Christian Europe. In many respects the material it contained was taken seriously, as were the words of the Holy Bible, and this included the accounts of sorcerous transformations.

An old folktale from Germany recounted in some versions of the *Malleus,* speaks of a woodcutter—a godly man—who, while out cutting trees on the edge of a forest near Strasburg, was attacked by three ferocious wildcats. Using his axe, he fought them off and managed to escape. Later, he approached a town where he was summarily arrested and held for three days without being told what crime he had committed. After the third day, he was taken to a house where several prominent women of the town lay ill, covered in blows and bruises, and he was told that all three had accused him of assaulting them. The man stood in astonishment, for the blows corresponded to the bodily areas where he had struck the wildcats with which he had fought earlier. He told the authorities his strange story, and, surprisingly, they believed him, for it had already been suspected that the three ladies had achieved their wealth and high social status by dark and dubious means. All the charges against him were instantly dropped and he was given a small amount of money to buy his silence. He was taken from the town without any further word of explanation. However, he stayed away from that area of the forest in case the witches might still be about in their wildcat guise.

Some French witch-hunters, followers of the intellectual Jean Bodin (1530–1596), who argued passionately for the belief in witchcraft, claimed that certain French witches could change shape by using strange and horrible ointments (some of which were said to contain the fat of dead, unbaptised children) into stoats, cats, and even dogs and wolves. In these guises they often robbed their neighbors and even carried away sleeping children from their cribs and beds for diabolical purposes.

Some scholars have argued, of course, that if these people smeared themselves with all sorts of questionable substances that were absorbed through the skin, that this may have produced some sort of hallucinatory state in which the subject only *imagined* that he or she was a wild animal. Or, such a belief may have emanated from a mental condition. Certainly the curious illusion of the woman who confessed to Bernardino of Sienna would seem to suggest this (she saw herself as a cat, but everyone else saw her as a human). Even so, the Church stated that there were indeed people who could transform themselves into animals, and most people (even the intellectuals of the day) did not dispute this.

Satanic Tranformations

It was also widely believed that servants of Satan could transform *others* into animals—against their will—if they so chose. Many writers, including those who compile the *Malleus*, firmly believed that Satan might give his servants powers to transform an individual into the guise of a beast or to make him or her adopt bestial characteristics. It was widely thought, for example, that local witches transformed their sleeping neighbors into the guise of horses and rode them all night, sometimes to the Sabbats (great gatherings of witches at which the Devil or his minions often appeared), returning them to bed, sweating and exhausted in the morning. In the Pendle area of Lancashire in 1612, for example, "Old Demdike" (Elizabeth Southerns)—one of the famous Pendle witches—was accused of turning enemies into hares. In parts of Germany and Northern Italy a number of witches were accused of turning neighbors into small horses and using them for ploughing. And local witches were not above changing their close relatives into animals as well.

In 1722 (although some sources give the date as 1727), Janet Horne of Dornoch in Sutherland, Scotland, was convicted and burned at the stake for allegedly turning her daughter into a pony and cantering her about the countryside. The girl had some kind of malformation (that she may have had since birth), which was attributed to witchcraft and transformations. In some of the accounts from Germany, relatives were sometimes transformed into horses or ponies, but also sometimes into wolves or bears, which also were said to serve as mounts for witches to ride to their diabolical gatherings.

All across medieval and early modern Europe the idea of certain people transforming themselves or being transformed into animals such as wolves was beginning to take hold of the collective mind, and an underlying ethical perception was being set too. Such transformations were usually not for the good of one's community—rather, they were almost invariably inspired by the forces of evil and maliciousness, perhaps to satisfy diabolical and unnatural lusts. Some of these transformations were into ferocious and unpredictable beasts, which might threaten society.

Leopard Men

So far we have looked at the notion of transformation from a western European and largely Christian perspective. However, the idea of transformation into beasts through supernatural means occurred in a number of other cultures as well.

Perhaps one of the best known ideas (and most frightening to Western eyes), is that of the Leopard Men of Africa, who could allegedly transform themselves into large and feral cats. Indeed, this was said to form the basis of an African cult, which was viewed in the same way that many Christian Westerners might view Voodoo in the Caribbean. This cult was said to have supernatural powers and could transform themselves into the form of animals at

meetings (not terribly far removed in the popular imagination from the Witches' Sabbats of western Europe) in order to do great wickedness both to neighboring peoples and to white settlers.

In antiquity, the leopard was a venerated animal, suggesting strength, swiftness, knowledge, and alertness. In Egypt, for example, it was used by certain pharaohs to symbolize their power and bravery in the face of their enemies, implying that some of the animal's supposed characteristics had somehow transferred themselves into the monarch.

In Africa, certain cults that flourished in the west (Sierra Leone, Cote d'Ivorie [Ivory Coast], Guinea, and Nigeria) were believed to carry on such veneration, but supposedly mixing it with other elements such as cannibalism and human sacrifice. Some of their victims, it was claimed, were young women who were sexually abused before being murdered.

It is possible that the Leopard Men may well have started out as a warrior cult among some of the tribes of west Africa. Similar to the berserkers in Scandinavia, young men may have been "possessed" by the leopard spirit in order to enable them to hunt with greater success or to oversee the social rites of passage for young men. It may then have developed into an almost clandestine society with wider supernatural implications. Shrines at which the cult assembled were erected to leopard gods deep in the forests, and their location was only known to trusted cult members.

The cult grouping was reputedly led by an individual known as the Bate Yele, who was the human embodiment of the leopard. He was dressed in a leopard skin and a leopard mask, sometimes with long bone or metal "claws," and he usually adopted the mannerisms and behavior of the animal in order to lead his followers. In some cases certain devotees of the cult would also don leopard skins and behave very much like leopards, claiming that they were "possessed" by the leopard spirit. It is also of note that the members of such cults were all male, and this has led to the assumption that it was in fact initially an exclusive "warrior" cult or even a "passage cult" (that is, marking the transition from boyhood to manhood). The Leopard Cult also functioned, to some extent, as the protector of the local community in which it flourished, and sometimes was also perceived as a possible conduit between men and the gods. If, for example, the crops failed, it was assumed that the gods were displeased in some way, and then the Leopard Cult might choose an individual from the local community to be sacrificed in order to assuage their anger. In this way, the crops flourished again and the community was saved from starvation.

Although the existence of the Leopard Men was already known, it first achieved prominence in the West around 1918 following a series of murders of young women in both Nigeria and Sierra Leone. Many of these murders were of colored women, but there were a couple of white women who were slain, which brought the cult to the attention of local administrators and subsequently to the world. It was viewed as a political movement against white Colonial administration and against the suppression of folk ways and beliefs among the indigenous population. Gruesome stories began to circulate regarding the atrocities of the cult. For example, it was widely stated that cult members cut out the intestines of the victims and boiled them into a porridge called *borfima*, which granted the drinker incredible supernatural powers and enabled him to transform into a leopard. There has never been any evidence for such a potion, but the idea of an evil cult of African nationalists lurking in the Western jungles was foremost in many Colonial minds.

It was directly after World War II, however, that the situation really intensified. In 1946 in Sierra Leone, Cote d'Ivorie, and Nigeria there were around 48 murders. Most of these killings appeared to have been carried out in ritualistic circumstances. The Colonial authorities began to take a much greater interest in the activities of the Leopard Cults, believing them to be politically motivated. This, of course, was at a time of a stirring African consciousness as exemplified by the Mau-Mau in Kenya. There were frequent arrests and interrogations as the authorities attempted to crack down on the cult.

This state of affairs carried into 1947 when there were several more murders, particularly in Nigeria, during the early months of the year. Between January and August, there were around 44 killings attributed to the Leopard Men, some involving white settlers. In eastern Nigeria, assistant commissioner Terry Wilson (who had only been in the position for six months) investigated, trying to find evidence against the cult. He and his men raided the house of a local witchdoctor named Nagogo (N'gogo), where he found a leopard robe, a leopard mask, and a two-pronged claw made of metal. He investigated further and found the remains of almost 15 bodies in various states of decomposition buried in the grounds not far from the house. All the bodies bore traces of ritual killing. Wilson immediately arrested Nagogo and threw him in jail awaiting trial. However, so feared were the Leopard Men that nobody would come forward to give evidence against him, and, although Nagogo confessed to being a member of a secret society, there was nothing to connect him directly with the murders. Fearing that the witch doctor was betraying their secrets, the cult suddenly turned on Nagogo's wife and daughters, brutally killing them. In a desperate attempt to get Nagogo to confess, Wilson showed him the mutilated bodies of some of the victims that had been dug up. The ordeal, coupled with the butchering of his family, proved too much for the man (who was quite elderly); he suffered a heart attack and died.

Wilson then flooded the area with more than 200 requested police officers in an attempt to track down cult members, without much success. It was widely believed that cult members could transform themselves into leopards and would hunt down those who informed against them. Wilson, however, decided to set a trap. He used one of his officers to pose as the son of a local woman in a village near where there had been a number of attacks, and to use a path where much evidence of the cult's activity had been noted. He then stationed a number of men in the bushes and waited. As the undercover policeman made his way along the forest path, he was suddenly attacked by a bizarre figure dressed in a leopard skin, wearing a mask and carrying a massive club. A fight ensued between the two men, but before reinforcements could arrive, the Leopard Man had crushed the policeman's skull with the club and had fled off into the thicket. However, it appeared that the policeman had given a good account of himself with a knife, and Wilson knew that he was looking for someone who was badly wounded. Nevertheless, after an initial search, found no one in the villages. Then he had another idea; he placed the dead constable's body in an open area of the main police compound, but kept it under strict surveillance. He was not to be disappointed. As night fell, a fantastic figure clad in leopard robes and carrying a great metal claw crept into the compound and began to attack the dead body by tearing out great chucks of bloody flesh. According to Wilson, the person behaved just as a leopard would. Walking toward the grizzly scene, he drew his pistol, and, as the Leopard Man reared up to attack, shot him in the chest. The Leopard Man fell dead. Now that locals saw that the Leopards were as human as themselves and could be killed like any other man, many came forward to inform and testify against them. In the last months of 1947 and into February 1948, Wilson and his men had arrested 73 cult members on the testimony of local chiefs. They had also uncovered a leopard shrine deep in the jungle. The shrine consisted of a large flat-shaped rock, deeply stained with human blood, a vast quantity of human bones, and a great effigy of a creature that was half-man, half-leopard. In mid-1948, 39 of the cult members were sentenced to death and hanged at Abak Prison. Although a major leopard cult had been smashed many other such grouping were said to exist in the west African provinces.

The story of the murders and the idea of a cult lurking somewhere in the African jungles whose members could transform themselves into leopards filtered back to Europe. It stirred up fears and anxieties concerning were-men and connected them in the Western perception almost inextricably with Paganism and evil. It was also linked in the 1950s and early 1960s with revolution and political strife, as a rising tide of "black consciousness" gripped some of the African countries, alarming the Colonial masters there. The specter of the African shapeshifting Leopard Man was perhaps just as potent a bogeyman as the wolf-man or werewolf in Medieval Europe. Similar to the wolf-man perhaps, it reminded civilized mankind of its feral and bloodthirsty aspect.

Lion Cults

The leopard was not the only terror to emerge out of Africa—in the central lands of the continent the lion cults flourished. In many respects these were similar to the Leopard Cults of western Africa and were just as ferocious. The lion, of course, had been accorded a special status in the common mind since earliest times. It was often associated with royalty and had been given the title "king of the beasts." Indeed, in ancient Egypt, lions were closely associated with the goddess Bastet or Sekhmet, who was depicted as having a lion's head as she sat on her throne. Also, large mummified cats have been found in certain important tombs such as Maia, the wet nurse to the boy pharaoh Tutankhamen.

The Greek historian Diodorus Siculus (first century BC) in his *Bibliotheca Historica* (supposedly a history of the entire world) writes in the third volume of the Kushites (southern Ethiopians) of Africa as being foremost among those who "venerated the lion." They were among the oldest indigenous peoples on the continent, and, consequently, their gods were some of the most ancient. One of their gods was Apedemek, who often took the form of a great lion. Apedemek descended from time to time, possessing certain rulers and issuing both instructions and prophesies to the Kushite people. The blood of the lion flowed in the veins of such rulers, and according to legend, it also transferred into those of some of the ancient Hebrews when the Queen of Sheba (who was of the Kushite line) became pregnant by King Solomon and gave birth to Menelek, from whom the former Ethiopian emperor Haile Selassie traced his line. He was also known as the "Lion of the South" or sometimes the "Lion of Judah," and is still venerated by the Rastafarian movement because of the lion's blood that was reputedly mingled with his own and which gave him his power and authority. Not only this, but in ancient Babylon, the lion was deemed to be the embodiment of the goddess Ishtar and conferred power on many ancient Babylonian rulers.

In the 1920s however, lion cults took on a relatively new and more sinister aspect. Around 1925, the British government of central Tanzania reported that some 200 people had lost their lives in the area of Singidia. At first marauding lions were suspected (many of the corpses were found in a mangled condition, as though they had been savaged by animals), but later this assumption was questioned. There were local stories in the region about a group of men who could transform themselves into lions and who worked with certain local witch doctors as assassins. A number of such killings continued well into the 1950s, rising to a peak around 1957. The killings were conducted very much in the style of those carried out by the Leopard Men and involved very small children—one little girl was torn from her mother's arms by a Lion Man who leapt out of the bushes dressed in a lion skin, and growled like a beast. Her dismembered body was found a little later out in the bush. There were also supposed to be blood-stained altars hidden away in remote Tanzanian valleys where human sacrifice was carried on in the most grotesque and stomach-churning ways. The lion cults were also rumored to exist in Zambia and Zaire where other ritual-style murders were committed. Indeed, in the Luapala Valley, which divides the two countries, lion cults were supposed to be extremely prolific. It was reputed that at certain altars concealed in the Valley, purification rites were carried out after local hunters slew a lion. This involved a shaman or witch doctor donning the hide of the slain lion and inviting its spirit to enter the human body, thus becoming temporarily one with the beast itself. The cults flourished, attracting Western attention and notoriety well into the 1960s, when they appeared to go underground again and disappeared. It is, of course, possible that they still flourish in some parts of Africa, even today.

Other Animal Cults

Other cultures, of course, had their own animal cults. Bear worship and possession by bear spirits was common among many Northern peoples, but especially amongst the Finns. Here, the bear was a central feature of several Finnish Pagan religions, which flourished long before the coming of Christianity. The early Finns viewed the bear as a celestial being with many supernatural powers, which had descended from the sky (some bear cults were even able to point out the Great Bear in the night sky as a place from where the holy creature had come) and therefore worthy of worship and attention. The spirit of the bear, it was said, resided in its skull and was known as *kallohonka*.

When the bear died or was killed, the spirit would transfer itself from the skull and into something else—a forest, a tree, a river, or even a human being. In this guise the kallohonka continued until it could be reincarnated as another bear. If it had entered the body of a human being, that individual might then take on the aspects and behavior of a bear. On high trees outside some Finnish villages, bear skulls were placed in the branches, so that the kallohonka might protect the locality and those that dwelt within the community. In some parts of Finland roughly a century ago, the bear was considered to be a physical manifestation of the sky-god Ukko, who alternated between an old man and a ferocious beast. The bear was also something of a totemic symbol in parts of Russia and among the Sami people (Lapland) where shamanism continued into the late 19th century. Similar to many witch doctors of old, Sami shamans sometimes supposedly took on the attributes of a bear to ensure success in the day's hunting. In order to affect this, the shaman was "possessed" by the spirit of the bear and aped ursine behavior and characteristics throughout the rituals that were performed in order to "draw down" good fortune.

There are also some evidences of bear cults—perhaps with totemic possessions among Neanderthal peoples (roughly 70,000 years ago) stretching back into prehistoric times. Neanderthal remains, coupled with those of cave bears found at Drachenloch (Dragon's Cave) in Switzerland between 1917 and 1921 are suggestive that some form of ancient veneration went on there, possibly involving totemic bear gods. Perhaps as with homo Sapiens, these were also hunting rituals.

In the Middle East, there are suggestions of ancient jackal cults, which probably had their origins in the Egyptian Old Kingdom (third millennium BC). The deity Anubis, prominent throughout the Old Kingdom, of course, sported a human body and the head of a jackal, and this idea was passed down into subsequent Middle Eastern cults in which dogs and jackals were venerated.

Both appear to have been closely associated with the dead. In some cases, mummified dogs have been found in certain tombs and jackals were seen scavenging in certain desert cemeteries. Indeed, the Pyramid Texts (the dynastic scrolls of the Old Kingdom from around the middle of the third millennium) attribute a certain degree of human intelligence to the jackal and identify the beast with certain rulers. The reference *may* be to an early jackal god named Apu, who was worshipped by the early Nile civilization and could, if he wished, take on human form. It is thought that some of the ancient Egyptian kings claimed to be the human incarnation of the god—combining in a sense both man and jackal. In some Arabic folklore, the jackal was connected in some unspecified way to the idea of the djinn—the formless spirits who came and went across the desert and who had supernatural powers. Some even claimed that jackals had once been human beings, changed into a canine form by these malignant forces either for their own amusement or out of spite. There were supposedly cults, dwelling in the wilds of the desert, who behaved like jackals and unquestionably attacked and killed any unfortunately traveler who accidentally strayed close to their domain.

But it is arguably from North American cultures that we perhaps have our most vivid picture of the shapeshifter. A belief in shapeshifting was known in America as far back as the ancient Mayan civilization (AD 250–900). In these cases, the concept closely parallels that of the *eigi einhamr* of the Norse tradition—that certain people can lay aside their natural skins and take on a new (unnatural) one—usually of some form of animal. In Guatemala and Honduras these individuals are still considered to be ferocious sorcerers, who generally use their powers for the detriment of society. They are sometimes known as *nawals* and were usually female (vicious, shape-changing wives who invariably practiced evil against their unfortunate husbands or sometimes their husband's families in their animal form). One of the favorite guises of the nawal was said to be that of a great dog or coyote—the belief probably deriving from the numbers of such creatures to be found wild in the countryside. In Indian folklore, in both North and South America, the coyote was regarded as something of a trickster and a creature that might lead humans from a virtuous path—something like certain types of fox in Japanese lore—and it was therefore not surprising that they should form part of the nawal tradition. In Mexico, these creatures were known as *nahaul* or *najual*, and had a pronounced preference for cheese and having sex with women when in a dog or coyote for.m They were also considered to be impervious to iron and to abhor human clothing.

North American Shapeshifters

It is perhaps among the North American native tribes that we are most familiar with the concept of shapeshifting from man to animal. The belief is known in a number of indigenous tribes including the Mohawk (whose territory once stretched from upstate New York to southern Quebec) where such individuals were known as *limmikin* and sometimes *yenaloosi*; branches of the Sioux, and the Apache. Among the most famous of the tribes in which the belief was prevalent were the Navajo, where they were often known as "skinwalkers," although this has to be seen within the overall context of (and as an attribute of) Navajo witchcraft. The Navajo name for such people is *yeenadlooshi*, which literally means "he goes on all fours," which gives the impression that at least some sort of "transformation" takes place, whether it be physical or behavioral. Skinwalkers, says Navajo tradition, are even physically different from ordinary people—the main difference being their eyes, which are large and luminous, even in daylight. Indeed, it is thought that to lock glances with a skinwalker enables him or her to absorb a victim into his or her own body and "steal their skin." It was extremely wise to avoid any eye contact with any person suspected of being a skinwalker.

In some versions of the tradition it is also said that their tongues would be black—another visible sign of their supposed witchcraft—and that their spittle was poisonous. Such people achieved the skinwalking status by breaking some form of cultural taboo or by direct contact with evil or malignant spirits through questionable behavior. Homosexuality, for example, was frowned on by Navajo society, and so anyone who practiced that (even in secret) was sure to attract dark forces and become a skinwalker. The shapeshifters took on a number of forms—owls, crows, beetles—but the most frequent were that of the coyote or the wolf. Both were regarded by the Navajo as cunning and ferocious creatures, and were often portrayed, in legend, as the enemies of mankind.

In the common mind, skinwalkers were generally perceived to be naked, as they took their supernatural form apart from some items of animal hide attached to them—for instance leggings, wristlets, or cloaks. They were believed to have no genitals, and their skin was reputedly rock-hard and impervious to arrows and axes. When they were in their animal form, it was said that most traces of human memory were gone and the instinct of the beast took over, rendering them vicious and unpredictable. They were also extremely agile and couldn't be caught, even by the most skillful hunter. Nevertheless, while in his or her bestial guise, the skinwalker could not fully imitate the walk or gait of the chosen creature, because in essence, he or she is human. In other versions among certain Navajo tribes, the intelligence and malevolence only increased, and when in their animal form, they were even able to read minds and to lure their victims from the safety of their homes by imitating the voices and cries of their loved ones.

Among the Christianised Navajo, there was a story that God had granted all men the power to transform themselves into the likeness of animals for protection, for use against enemies, or in order to do good. Gradually, because man did not follow God's Commandments, he gradually took the power away from the wider world, but he left it with the Navajo, although only a few now seem to have it—and some of those use it for evil. Some Navajo voluntarily gave up the power, but others hid it and used it for their own benefits. Others claimed, of course, that the powers came from the Pagan Devil, and were only used by his servants. Nowadays it is difficult to know if the skinwalking belief survived, because even today it is perceived as being tied up with Navajo witchcraft, and those who talk about it may fear supernatural retribution by witches.

Werewolves

Among the Hopi Indians (Arizona, Utah, and Colorado), skinwalking is conferred on sorcerers through a special ceremony known as Ya-Ya, details of which are extremely secret and well-protected, but it is thought to involve donning the skins of the animal that the individual wishes to become. Many scholars believe that such a ceremony has its roots far in the prehistoric past; anthropologist A.M. Stephenson has suggested that it may come from a very old Hopi word *yaa-yuutu* meaning "mother." The ceremony was reputedly conducted under the auspices of the god Ponochon (meaning "sucks from the belly") and was associated with a particular star in the heavens (which some have identified with the star Sirius—the Dog Star). It was also said to involve walking through hot fire and a test for seeing things far away (as an animal might). If the individual was able to see these things it was a sure sign that he had become a were-creature. Much of the ritual was designed to invite the animalistic spirit people down from the Heavens to "possess" the person concerned, ostensibly for the good of the tribe (perhaps through hunting). However, much of this remains speculation and there is little evidence for any of these claims. The ceremony, if it is still carried out, remains a closely guarded secret of the Hopi people.

In very early times, the distinction between man and beast was not always so clear-cut as it is today. Men hunted alongside the animals and battled against them for prey; perhaps some of our early ancestors' behavior reflected that of our bestial partners. Cannibalism may have flourished in earlier societies, as did beast-like frenzies in times of battle and war. Memories of this may have continued down in human consciousness through myth, tradition, and legend. As well as admiring the skill, cunning, and prowess of the animals, mankind was always well aware of its own darker side. There was also the fear of the unknown—what lay out there in the dark beyond the friendly glow of the campfire or beyond the shores of well-known lands.

As human culture began to develop, human imagination sought to imbue such far-away and possibly dangerous places with all manner of monsters including dog-heads and other such creatures. Travelers from abroad strove to interpret what they had seen in foreign parts—the great apes, the baboons, and the mandrills—in a way that would make sense both to themselves and to those to whom they told their journeys. To do this, they invoked the idea of the beast-man, somewhere between man and animal, who combined elements of both. The image of the feral man, living out in the wild just beyond the borders of civilization was an extremely potent one, and took hold of the popular imagination. And what creature was more savage or feral than mankind's oldest competitor—the wolf? In many cultures it is the canine that often becomes the subject of many of these strange transformations, for the age-old question remained buried somewhere deep in the human psyche: What if a man could transform himself into the guise of a wolf? The template of the werewolf belief that would be subsequently handed down to us was already being laid.

3

Old Irish Wolves and Other Wonders

'Tis like the howling of Irish wolves against the moon.

—William Shakespeare, *As You Like It*

As with early vampire tales, one of the oldest written stories concerning werewolves comes from Ireland. Written around 1185 by the Welsh monk Giraldus Cambrensis (Gerald of Wales), who had come to Ireland as part of the retinue of Prince John (made Lord of Ireland by his father—the English king Henry II), the *Werewolves of Ossory* is a typical medieval ecclesiastical tale, emphasising the power of the Church and the need for Salvation. Both of Gerald's own maternal and paternal relatives, the

Fitzgeralds and the Fitzstephens, held lands in what are now Counties Kildare and Wexford in Ireland, and it was from them that Giraldus heard a number of old tales that he unquestioningly accepted and faithfully recounted. He compiled an "early travel book" on the country—the *Topographica Hibernica* (*A General History and Topography of Ireland*), which would remain as a reference for travelers until the 1600s. This was a mixture of geographical description of areas of Ireland (some of which Giraldus had never seen, but had learned of only by hearsay), and some wonderous stories that were circulating at the time. He accepted all of these stories recording them as if they were indisputable fact. He believed almost everything that he was told. Among these tales was one concerning the Werewolves of Ossory.

Wolf Breeds

Up until the 18th century (and maybe even after) Ireland always had a problem with wolves. During the medieval and early modern periods, the country was largely covered by thick and almost impenetrable forest, which made it an ideal breeding and hunting place for the animals. Indeed, so acute was the problem that the name of the wolf was incorporated into the breed of a certain dog, which was supposedly used to hunt them—the Irish wolfhound. The name *Irish wolfhound* is probably something of a misnomer, because the dogs are not native to the island, but were probably imported from England during Roman times. There is a Roman bronze of a very similar hound from Lydny in Gloucestershire (known as the "Lydny Hound") dating from around AD 365 and there are references to a temple of Nodens somewhere in England (the exact location is not specified) where special dogs licked the wounds of the sick or injured in order to produce a cure. Such hounds were considered to be guard dogs or war dogs, and it is possible that the animals were imported into Ireland by the Celts in order to deal with a growing problem of wolves.

Wolves in the Wild

Ireland appears to have been overrun with wolves right up until the late 1700s, many of which seem to have been extremely ferocious—especially during the harsh winter months. For example, in 1596, Lord William Russell records in his diary that he and Lady Russell were able to go wolf hunting in November in the woods around Kilmainham (near Dublin), and as late as 1650, the town of Coleraine in County Derry was attacked by a starving wolf pack during a particularly severe winter. Around the same time there are reports of travelers being attacked by wild wolves around the towns of Lisburn and Drogheda and along the shores of Lough Neagh. In 1652, at Kilkenny, Oliver Cromwell issued a prohibition forbidding the export of Irish wolfhounds, so great was the wolf problem in the country. In 1669, an early guidebook entitled *The Travels of Cosmo* described Ireland as "Wolfland." As late as 1750, there were tales of marauding packs of wolves in Wexford and parts of County Cork. The last two wolves in Ireland were reputedly killed in the Wicklow Mountains around 1770, by a wolf-hunter who supposedly went by the name of Rory Carragh (some other versions state that Carragh was no more than a simple shepherd), who, together with a small boy, tracked them to a ruin where they had made their den. Although these were supposedly the very last wolves, there are nevertheless reports of the creatures in Ireland right up until the early years of the 1800s in places such as Tyrone, though these have not been verified. It is therefore appropriate that Ireland serves as the location for one of the first recorded werewolf tales.

The First Tale

The incident, according to Giraldus Cambrensis, supposedly occurred only a few years before the arrival of Prince John in Ireland. A certain unnamed priest was traveling from Ulster to Meath on a matter of some ecclesiastical importance. He was accompanied on his travels by a small boy. During the journey the pair spent the night in a particularly dark and threatening wood on the edge of the ecclesiastical See of Ossory. As they lay down to sleep in the dark, the priest was suddenly disturbed by a human voice calling to him from the nearby forest. Rising, he walked to the edge of the circle of firelight and looked out into the gloom. As a huge wolf came padding into the light the priest drew back in terror, shielding the boy behind him from the animal. The wolf spoke to him in human tones, and told him not to be afraid. The creature wasn't really a wild animal, but one of a clan from the district who had been cursed by an irascible saint named St. Natalis, a rather moody holy man. Every seven years two of their clan had to assume the shape of wolves and go to live in the forest. At the end of seven years they returned to their clan, resumed human form, and two more took on the wolf guise. The last couple—a husband and wife—who had taken the wolf-shape were quite old, and the forest life hadn't really agreed with them. The wolf who now spoke was the old man; his wife was quite ill and was probably going to die. The male wolf had come to seek out a priest to give her the last rites and make her peace with God. The wolf therefore asked the priest to come with him and administer the Holy Sacrament. The holy man considered this strange request, but agreed, although the wolf insisted that he come alone and leave the boy by the fire. Reluctantly, the priest followed the creature into the depths of the wood, and eventually they reached a den at the foot of a great tree. There lay a she-wolf, obviously close to death. The cleric approached her with some trepidation, and, turning to his guide, asked the animal if there was some proof that this was indeed an old woman and not a savage forest creature. The wolf replied that if the priest drew his knife and cut part of the she-wolf's skin, he would receive his proof. The cleric cut a slit into the belly of the she-wolf. He was shocked to see the face of an elderly woman looking out at him, and realized that what the wolf said was true. Without hesitation, he administered the blessing, and the old woman expired peacefully. The wolf guided him back to his fire as morning approached, and, after making several prophesies about the continuation of the English in Ireland, disappeared back into the woodlands. The priest promised to visit him again when he returned from his business in Meath, but despite his promise, he never saw the wolf again.

The story, taken as true, seems to have caused some consternation in the Irish clergy. Two years afterward, Giraldus was in the same area, where he was approached by two priests at the behest of a local bishop asking him for his views on this "serious matter." Giraldus met with the bishop and a small synod and gave his views in writing. These writings formed the basis of a sealed report, which was sent through the Bishop of Ossory directly to Pope Urban III. Whether or not the Pope had actually requested the report from the Irish clergy is not a matter of record. However, the act shows the seriousness with which the matter was viewed, and the report is thought not to have dealt with the factuality of the tale, but rather its theological implications.

Ancient Questions

These questions were well-founded, for in the late medieval period (when Giraldus was writing) there were a number of challenges to the established

order of things. It was an age of great scholasticism, and thinkers were once again rediscovering the philosophical works of ancient Greece and Rome, particularly Aristotle, who in his *Physica* queried the ordered structure of the universe. Such theories bordered on heresy, but they set churchmen thinking. Following some of this early speculation, the boundaries between humans and the world around them became less sure. Could man somehow be transformed into animals as legend suggested, or even into stone as some myths hinted? What was the real difference among men, animals, and stones? If man reflected God's glory, then so did the rest of the world, and was it not possible that one part might transform itself into another? So great was the speculation in monkish circles that in Switzerland, Conrad, Bishop of Hersiau, forbade his brethren even to discuss the possibility or read treatises on the subject—especially Ovid's *Metamorphosis*, on pain of instant excommunication.

Metempsychosis

In this context, very ancient theories about the nature of the world were starting to re-emerge during this period. One of these was the notion of *metempsychosis*, which was said to have "originated" with the Greek philosopher Pherecydes (although some say it was an even older form of thinking that had come from Egypt). It had been elaborated by his pupil Pythagoras, who had a direct implication for Church teaching. This theory dealt with the transmigration of souls from one form into another—from the human to the animal, the plant to the stone—and threatened to break down the very barriers between the facets of Creation, which the Church said God had established. It was a small wonder that high churchmen such as Conrad denounced and forbade all reading and discussion concerning it.

Millenarians

There was yet another idea that influenced to this theory of mutability. Many people believed that the world was in its end times, and that Christ was coming once again to judge it and establish a New Kingdom on earth. This was supposed to happen in the year 1000—obviously it didn't, but millenarian thinking was still prevalent at many levels of society. When he came, he would gather the righteous and the blessed to him, and would transform them from their corrupt fleshly bodies into something else more wonderful. This idea of transformation with its new and altered body in the New Kingdom permeated medieval religious thinking at a fundamental level, and has even continued down through some Millenarian fundamentalist cults until the present day. This of course fed into wider communal thinking, and imaginations were filled with green men, werewolves, and dreams of alchemy against which the Church took an outraged stance.

There was, however, a flaw in the Church's argument concerning metempsychosis. At the heart of Christian ritual lay the Mass, and that rite involved the mystery of transubstantiation. It was part of Church teaching that when the Eucharist was placed on the tongue of the supplicant, it became the actual physical body of Christ, and that when the wine was drunk, it became his blood. In other words, under God's power, the bread and wine were transformed into something else that was the essence of the living, breathing Jesus. This was the very core of Christian belief, and although the Protestants would later rail at the belief, it has continued to be so until now. The Church could hardly argue against *mutato* (as it referred to the transmigration of the soul) if it continued to hold such a similar central theory. It was a serious problem for Church teachers, and so Giraldus's story about men changing into wolves was a highly controversial one.

As part of the tale, in subsequent editions of the *Topographica,* Giraldus also includes a long and rather rambling exposition of the underlying elements. This may be part of the sealed report that he sent to Pope Urban. In it, he tried to debate the story within an academic and ecclesiastical context (ineffectively, it has to be said). He draws attention to one of the transubstantive miracles of Christ—namely the changing of the water into wine at the wedding feast in Canaan of Galilee, the miracle of transubstantiation, and the transfiguration of Christ. The result is, however, pretty inconclusive.

Other Legends

The alleged experiences and testimony of the priest involved are also inconclusive. Although trying to rationalize the account in theological terms, Giraldus completely accepts the encounter as true. The priest is not identified, nor is his mission in County Meath ever specified; it is reasonable to suppose that he was perhaps a local cleric who may not have traveled all that far. What he may have given was a hysterical, disjointed account that subsequent recountings forged into something of the coherent story that Giraldus wrote down as fact. But did he actually encountered a talking wolf? Not only did the woodlands of Ireland teem with such animals, but, similar to parts of England, they also held wild and wolfish men as well. Similar to the berserkers, some of these men wore wolfskins, almost as part of a uniform. These men were extremely dangerous, functioned mainly as outlaws, and were often known as "wood-kern" (wood soldiers) or "faelad" (wolf-like or wild men). The name held echoes of the legendary Laignech Faelad or "the Wolf Men of Tipperary" whom William Camden so mockingly dismissed in the 16th century.

What if the priest had encountered one of these outlaws, dressed in wolfskins, and his subsequent garbled account of the incident had been misinterpreted and exaggerated? Similar to "Chinese whispers," the story grew and changed with its circulation within the community, and the wild man of the tale became an actual wolf. The faelad were considered to be fervently anti-English (they were thought to be remnants of old Irish woodsmen who had dwelt in the forests before the coming of the Normans to Ireland), and the prophesies of the wolf and the ousting of the English from the country would seem to support this. It is possible that the "wolf" may have been an outlaw. This is something that Giraldus and other churchmen did not consider. The story, however, both fit in with and contributed to the mood of the times and located the idea of the werewolf firmly in Ireland.

French Tales

But Ireland was not the only country to concern itself with werewolves or wolf-men in medieval times. Brittany, France, also appears to have had a similar tradition. This appears in the writings of a 12th-century French poet living in England named Marie de France (Mary of France). From the court of Henry II, where she may have been a noblewoman serving the King's wife, Eleanor of Aquitaine (there are suggestions that she might have been King Henry's illegitimate half-sister), she wrote a number of lais (short narrative poems), one of which contains a tale about a werewolf. Although the original text was written in French, it was subsequently translated by monks into Anglo-Saxon English, and there may have been some additions and modifications during this process. Little is known about Marie's life; however, it is thought that she had an interest in old folktales—both morality stories and otherwise—and ancient wonder stories (she also translated a number of *Aesop's Fables*), and used them as part of her work. The lai concerning the werewolf Bisclavret, which has the feeling of a traditional tale from Brittany, may be one such story.

Bisclavret

The story involves a noble baron in Brittany—Bisclavret—who disappeared into the forest for three days every week without anyone knowing where he was going. His wife grew curious about his movements and begged the baron to tell her where he went and what he did. Bisclavret confessed that he was a werewolf and went to hunt in wolf form in the woodlands, leaving his clothes at the very edge of the forest. Without these clothes, he could not change back into human form. However, Bisclavret's wife was unfaithful, and had a secret lover who was a local knight. Armed with this information, they followed the baron to the woods, and when Bisclavret removed the clothing and assumed his wolf form, they gathered up the discarded garments and returned with them to the castle. Bisclavret was permanently trapped in the wolf guise. The unfaithful wife told everyone that the baron must have been killed, so she and her lover married and took over Bisclavret's lands.

Some time after, the king (who was Bisclavret's friend) and his retinue were hunting in the forest and the royal hounds managed to corner a wolf. Recognizing the monarch, Bisclavret, the wolf ran to seize his stirrup and kiss his foot—much to the astonishment of everyone. The king ordered his hounds to stand off; he took the wolf back to the palace as his pet. The wolf was so kind and gentle that it became a great favorite at the court. However, when the knight who married Bisclavret's wife appeared, Bisclavret attacked him. A wise man at the court declared that this was out of character for the animal, and something about the knight provoked it. Shortly after, the king visited Bisclavret's wife, who greeted him fondly, but the wolf, who is with the monarch, attacked the woman and bit off her nose. This raised further queries, and the king ordered the knight and his partner to be "put to the question" (that is, tortured). At this the wife promptly confessed and showed everyone Bisclavret's clothes. The wolf was then shown the clothes, but ignored them until the wise

man stated that he should be allowed to transform back to a human guise in private; Bisclavret once again regained his true form. The monarch restored him to his lands and exiled the knight and the unfaithful wife. All the children who were thereafter born to the unfaithful wife had no noses, a reminder of how she had dealt with Bisclavret.

There are a number of intriguing aspects to the tale, not least of all the hero's name. The word *Bisclavret* is a compound Breton linguistic form—"bisc" (short) and "lavret" (wearing breeches). This would seem to suggest that the wearing of clothes was important; somehow, the donning of garments marked the civilized man from the actual beast, which went naked. Other linguists have pointed to another possible meaning also taken from the Breton—*bleize lavaret* or "speaking wolf" in which case the notion of the clothing did not assume such a central role.

The creature that Bisclavret became was not known as a werewolf, but as a "garwolf," which was a French Norman name for a "man wolf." This was not exactly the ferocious creature with which we are all so familiar, but rather a man who took on the shape of a wolf for specific purposes (for example, hunting), but who was essentially human in nature. He had all the human faculties and tended to think like a man while having the natural skills and abilities of a beast. In fact, some of the individuals concerned, who were garwolves, spent equal periods of time as a man and as an animal.

Melion

The lai became highly popular at both the French and English courts, and may have formed the basis for a later story that was also current in England throughout the late 12th and early 13th centuries. The author of this tale is unknown, but it originated in Picardy somewhere between 1190 and 1204 and was carried around from fair to fair by jongulars (wandering entertainers), who made it extremely popular. Initially, the story also had strong French connections and concerned a noble named Melion, who might well have been Breton. Later interpretations made him a knight at the Court of King Arthur, famed throughout the land as a powerful and successful hunter, although nobody knows the secret of his hunting skills. Desirous of a wife, he searches through the court, but can find no suitable woman. One day, while out hunting, he is approached by a rather grand lady who announces that she is the daughter of the King of Ireland and that she has loved Melion from afar for years. Finally, she persuaded her father to allow her to come to England to marry him because she will take no other husband. Impressed by her regal manner, Melion agrees. The two married and the woman bears him two children. However, she would be as unfaithful as Bisclavret's wife, and had another plan in mind.

Out hunting again, Melion's party seems to disturb a stag that has been grazing among some rushes. The lady, who is with the group, states that she must have the meat of the animal and will not eat anything unless Melion places it before her. Sending his companions away, the knight finally shows her the secret of his hunting prowess. If he is touched while naked, by the white stone of a ring that he wears, he will be transformed into the likeness of a wolf, and this way he can hunt his prey easily. Only by donning his clothes once more can he transform himself back into a human. The lady begs him to become a wolf and capture the stag for her, so he strips down, she touches him with the stone from the ring, and he becomes a wolf. Once he is in animal form, however, the lady gathers up the clothes, takes the ring, and absconds with the squire, leaving Melion behind. For some time Melion lives in the forest as a wild animal; however, hearing that his wife has returned to Ireland, he manages to stow away on a ship bound for that country. However, he is soon discovered, and is abused by the crew because of his lupine form. Arriving in Ireland, Melion teams up with several other wolves, and together they attack sheep until the Irish king and his knights hunt them down, killing all the others, but leaving Melion alone.

Shortly after, King Arthur arrives from Britain with his retinue and takes up residence in an uninhabited castle at the very edge of the forest. Hearing that the English king is there, Melion goes to meet him. In his wolf form he runs up and licks the monarch's stirrup. Surprised and delighted by this "tame wolf," Arthur accepts the beast into his court. However, among the company, Melion recognizes the squire who has run away with his wife, and, in anger, attacks him. The king is greatly surprised at the behavior of the normally placid animal and questions (tortures) the squire, who eventually confesses all. The faithless wife is summoned by her father and brings with her the ring and clothes, which will restore Melion to human form. Back as a noble, Melion briefly considers punishing his wife and the squire by turning them both into wolves, but in the end decides against it and returns to England with Arthur where he lives an untroubled life.

Human and Animal Worlds

Both of the previous stories are deemed to come from Brittany, and both show man-animal motifs, common in other Celtic tales. The Celtic mind, which often saw men as the embodiment of (and at one with) their environment made little distinction between humans and beasts. Men and animals seemed to interchange with a surprising regularity and seemingly without much thought. Also, many of them seemed to have the same underlying message and motifs—the faithless partner, some token that can return the protagonist back to human form, and the quest to find true love. Interestingly, humans appear to be put off by taking animals as partners.

For example, in "The Hoodie's Bride," a story collected in the Cowal Peninsula in the West of Scotland by Scottish folklorist John Campbell in the late 1800s (a story that bears some resemblance to Bisclavret), a farmer's daughter marries a hoodie (a hooded crow or raven) and returns with him to his own country. He gives her the choice of seeing him as a hoodie during the day and as a man at night or visa versa, and she chooses to have him as a human during the day. She bears him a child, and when it is one year old, hoodies (her husband's people) arrive one night and carry it away from its crib. The wife is distraught, but her husband comforts her and tells her that it is the way of his people. She bears him a second child and the same thing happens. Again the woman is comforted by her husband, but when a third child is stolen away, she insists that he go to his people (the hoodies) and demand the return of all the children. Reluctantly he agrees, but he does not return. It is thought that once he is back among his kind, he has forgotten his life in the human world.

Werewolves

His wife sets out to find him and ventures deep into the country of the hoodies. At last she gains news of her husband—he is to marry again. The lady in question lives in a very grand house, and the hoodie's wife manages to get a job there as a servant. On the day of the wedding there is a great meal prepared and she must serve it. She will directly serve her husband, who sits at the head of the table. She has in her pocket a feather from his tail when he was in his hoodie form. This she slips onto the serving plate in order to remind him. His new wife glimpses it, realizes what is going on, and tries to prevent him from seeing it. Three times she returned the plate using some pretext, but in the end, the wife slipped the feather into a bowl of broth and was able to serve it up to her husband. The man saw the feather and remembered who he was and also remembered his wife. The pair left the land of the hoodies and returned to the human world where they lived in happiness thereafter. (In some variants of the story their children were restored to them.)

The story contains many of the elements common in other such tales from the Celtic tradition in which the protagonist slips easily between the world of the humans and the animal world. However, there is an added factor that distinguishes this tale from the likes of Bisclavret and Melion: the element of forgetting a previous life. Bisclavret and Melion are *garwolves*—thinking, fully cognizant creatures—who remember their past human lives and who recognize their former acquaintances. In both cases they run to acknowledge their king. The hoodie, on the other hand, instantly forgets his life among humankind (even when he is in human form) as soon as he returns to "his own people," and when his former wife appears before him as a servant, he does not recognize her. It is only when he sees a token from his bestial self in the form of a feather (which his people try to conceal from him) that he actually remembers who he is.

The story that Campbell collected in Scotland is thought to have been extremely old—dating back perhaps to medieval times. As such, it may very well belong to the Celtic cycles that include Bisclavret and Melion. It also represents, however, a move away from the "thinking and cultured animal" of Norman and medieval legend toward the more ferocious and savage type of creature (*le bete sauvage*) found in many of the more recent werewolf tales.

Gorlagon

Before leaving the corpus of Celtic tales from the medieval period, it is perhaps worth mentioning the tale of Gorlagon, which, although assumed to be Welsh in origin, appears in Latin. It may have been a part of what might be described as the "Arthur cycle"—a number of informal legends and folktales involving King Arthur. In some aspects, the tale bears a distinct resemblance to some of the Breton stories, which were circulating at this time, and may indeed have been influenced by them. One of the versions of the tale dates from around the 14th century, and though displaying all the attributes of courtly romance, it still boasts much of its Celtic flavor and origins.

In this version, Arthur is challenged by his queen to discover the nature and ways of a woman. This is a daunting quest for any knight, but Arthur accepts the challenge and sets out alone. He rides to the castle of a neighboring king named Gargol. This king, he finds, cannot help him, but directs him to another location—the castle of his brother, King Torleil. However, the second king is of no more help than the first, so, following even more directions, Arthur is forced to continue his quest to the stronghold of a third royal brother, King Gorlagon. Here, at last, the king tells him a tale that will answer at least a part of his quest, although Gorlagon warns him that the answers he receives will only marginally satisfy him.

Werewolves

The story concerns a king in a foreign land who had a garden that grew a magic sapling. Whoever cut this sapling, struck his head three times with it, and repeated a certain formula, would become a wolf. The king's wife discovered the secret of the sapling, cut it down, and used it to transform her husband into a beast, which she then drove from the court. Claiming that the king was dead, she then married the youngest son of a Pagan king and ruled the country with him. The transformed king fled into the forest, where he lived, met a she-wolf, and soon raised a family of his own. However, he still harbored great resentment toward his former wife.

Eventually, he, his wolf-wife, and their young entered a nearby town and attacked a number of people including two princes, who were the sons of his former wife and her new husband. The wolves were driven off by the citizens of the town, but returned to attack two nobles—both local counts and cousins of the queen—during which some of their young were captured and subsequently killed.

Driven mad with grief at the loss of his offspring, the werewolf now attacked the flocks and herds of farmers until he was run across the border into another province, where he was not welcome. Eventually, he went to live in a large stretch of forest, far away from his original home. There, overhearing a conversation between two peasants, he learned that the king of that area planned to hunt him down and kill him. He therefore decided to regain his human form once more, and in order to bring this plan about, he waylaid the king while he was out riding. As with the Bisclavret story, he ingratiated himself with the monarch and persuaded the king not to slay him; he gradually became a royal favorite much admired by the Court. However, he did not get on so well with the king's wife, who was secretly conducting an affair with one of the servants. When her husband was away, she mistreated the wolf and stirred up its resentment. As she was engaged in love-making, the beast pounced

and inflicted grievous wounds on the servant in question. Taking advantage of the situation, the queen had her own son locked away in a dungeon and declared that the wolf had eaten him while in a wild state, even though the brave servant had tried to defend him. The wolf, however, managed to entice the king to follow him down to the dungeon where the boy was discovered alive and unharmed. The servant eventually confessed what had truly happened, and was flogged for his crime; the queen was publicly torn limb from limb by horses.

Following this dreadful occurrence the king voiced his suspicions that the wolf appeared to be so intelligent that it might indeed be a man in another guise. In response to this suggestion, the wolf licked his hand and the monarch knew it was true. The king decided that he would follow wherever the wolf would lead him, and find out the source of this apparently enchantment. The werewolf led him back to its native country where they discovered that the whole land was languishing under the most fearful tyranny in the absence of its true ruler. Making a quick decision, the king invaded and won a great victory, deposing the tyrant and his wife. The wolf then took them to the garden where the magic sapling had grown, and he forced the defeated wife to bring another such sorcerous growth in order to restore the werewolf to human shape.

After King Gorlagon tells Arthur the story, Arthur is very taken with it. However, he has a question to ask the strange king: He espied an eerie and somber-looking woman who sat all alone in a corner of the castle holding a bloody head upon a platter, which she kissed whenever Gorlagon kissed his wife. Arthur wished to know who she was. The monarch explains that this is the unfaithful queen who turned the king into a wolf, for *he* was that werewolf, and *he* spared her life on the condition that she would always carry the head of her former lover with her in order to be reminded of her wickedness.

Linguistic students, when considering this tale, have pointed out that the name *Gorlagon* is an expanded form of *Gorgol*, which in Old Welsh (the story is believed to be Welsh in origin) means werewolf. This version of the tale comes from the 13th or 14th century, and has been added to in order to incorporate some form of courtly status and connection to Arthurian Romance. However, it is in all probability a much older tale. Again, there is a move away from the gentle, holy wolf that graces Giraldus's tale, and a much more savage beast, which attacks and kills young princes and devours sheep and cattle. True, there are barbarous elements in the original tale, but these seem to have been exaggerated in order to shock and disturb the late medieval, courtly mind. This once more strengthens the template for the werewolf that we both recognize and fear.

The Romance of Guillaume de Palerne

A much more complex and slightly different version of the Celtic motifs previously mentioned was also circulating at the time, and it is worth examining this story as a possible counterpoint to the core themes of the previous tales. This could be the most circulated version of all the werewolf stories, and, although originally written (it is assumed) in the late 12th century in Old French, perhaps the best-known version is in translated Middle English from the late 15th or early 16th centuries. In fact, it would appear to have been printed by the early English printer Wynkyn de Worde, who was a successor to the celebrated William Caxton, described as the father of English printing. It is thought that de Worde used an Irish translation of the tale, which was available around the 1520s, rather than a French variant. The tale, however, is French, and was known as *The Romance of Guillaume de Palerne*. Indeed, a French edition of the tale was printed in Lyon in 1552 and was widely circulated, establishing once and for all the werewolf legend in the common mind. An addendum to the prose text states that it initially came from an old Latin manuscript, giving it a greater authenticity and gravitas.

The tale is set, not in Ireland, Scotland, Wales, or France (which were the normal Celtic locations), but in "The Kingdom of the Two Sicilies" (that is, the island of Sicily and Southern Italy, which were under a unified administration). The region had been formerly invaded by the Saracens, but had been taken over by a concerted Norman advance by the beginning of the 12th century. A consolidated Sicilian Norman kingdom had been established, jointly ruled by the Counts of Calabria and Apulia (Italy) and the Kings of Sicily (who were distantly related).

The story is an incredibly complex one of which the werewolf motif is only a part. The werewolf in question is actually Alphonse, a son of the king of Spain, who had been spitefully transformed into the shape of a wolf by his stepmother, who is a witch. She smears him with an enchanted ointment, changing him to a beast, and then tells everybody that he has drowned. A little later, the werewolf rescues the son of the king of Sicily, who is named Guillaume, from a plot to take his life (according to some variants of the story, he would later become William I of Sicily). Pursued by murderous nobles, he flees across Sicily, and escapes by swimming across the Straits of Messina to the mainland bearing the child on his back. He leaves the child with some shepherds, who raise him as their own—however, he is later found by the Roman emperor and is taken back to the Imperial Palace. There, he falls in love with the emperor's daughter, Melior, but their love is forbidden, so the couple elopes, aided by the werewolf. They hide in the forest where the werewolf brings them food and drink and later disguises them so that they can travel about, first dressed in bear-skins and later in the hides of two deer, which the wolf has caught. Returning to Sicily, they are almost caught when soldiers climb onto the barge where they are hiding, but the werewolf distracts them by leaping in the water. Eventually, Guillaume is able to defeat his enemies and reclaim his father's throne. The werewolf, Alphonse, is finally returned to human shape and marries Guillaume's sister. His wicked stepmother repented (perhaps under encouragement from the new king) and put a red cord, complete with an enchanted ring, around the werewolf's neck and read out the appropriate magical spells from her book. When Alphonse resumes human form, he is found to be naked, and the queen then has to bathe him and find human clothes for him before the disenchantment is complete.

In this tale, the werewolf is not really the central character—that is Guillaume—but appears like a guardian angel or fairy godmother when danger threatens or items are needed for survival. He is the very epitome of the "thinking wolf," and shows little of the savagery that we often associate with the creature. Indeed, he only shows his savage side twice during the entire tale: when he attacks his wicked stepmother immediately after his transformation and just before his transformation back to human. These two outbursts of savagery are perhaps quite understandable given the circumstances. Far from being a being of evil, or being in league with the Devil, the werewolf appears almost saintly. And this theme seems to recur in all the early medieval tales. Though in the guise of an animal, the werewolf is, in effect, the very epitome of morality—the noble creature rising above the often wicked humans.

However, as Western civilization began to expand into previously unknown areas of the world, the idea of monstrous races and ghostly creatures began to take great prevalence and to absorb the cultured mind. The idea of terrible, threatening beings lurking in other parts of the earth seemed to grip the human imagination and provided speculative food for thinkers. Such thinking would soon encompass the werewolf.

Man-Ox

Returning to Giraldus and his book on Ireland, one of the popular stories that he retold as fact was that of a man-ox living in the Wicklow Mountains. There is no suggestion that Giraldus had ever seen the man-ox (indeed, it is thought that he arrived in Ireland shortly after the creature had died), but he probably heard the story from his kinsmen, the Fitzgaralds, who held lands in Wicklow. Indeed, during the latter days of his time in Ireland Giraldus is known to have stayed at the court of his cousin Maurice Fitzgerald, where such tales were probably common. Nor does Giraldus attribute any malignity to the were-ox, but rather treats it as a "wonder," and a curiosity. Similar to many other medieval writers, he describes it in detail.

The man-ox had hooves instead of hands and feet, and was able to feed itself by holding food in its forelegs and bringing it to its mouth. It had huge eyes similar to that of common oxen, but no nose—just two nostrils in the middle of a flat face. Its head was entirely bald, but was covered in some sort of soft, downy fur. The creature could not speak in human tongue, but made harsh lowing noises in order to communicate. According to Giraldus, the were-ox had been brought to Maurice Fitzgerald's court where it had proved to be a wonder to all who saw it. It does not really occur to the monk that this might have been a human being with grotesque deformities, and it shows how the idea of the monstrous was gradually creeping into human interpretations, even at this early time. Giraldus also mentions another story that he had heard in

Wicklow concerning a "man-calf," which had been born to a cow in the mountains, somewhere near the monastic city of Glendalough, in what was considered among the Norman nobles to be a fairly backward part of the region—"where the Irish had their habitations."

This monstrous birth, Giraldus confidently asserted, was the result of sin, the perceived "Irish custom" of having sex with livestock and animals in the wild. Indeed many of these monstrous "wonders" were sometimes used by monkish medieval writers to reinforce morality and to rail against sexual congress with beasts. If they are to be believed, then the "terrible sin" of bestiality seems to have been more widespread than originally thought. Of course this was in direct contravention to the Holy Law laid down in Leviticus 20:16—"If a woman approaches any beast to have intercourse with him; ye shall kill the woman and let the beast die the death." It was to be counted as a "most grievous" sin. This teaching added a new dimension to the idea of monsters. No longer were they to be found solely in foreign lands, but they might emerge from time to time closer to home as the result of sexual sin. In this, it "personalized" the idea of such creatures—any one of us could become a monster by disobeying God's laws.

Were-Sheep and Other Sins

A famous example of such a "monster" occurred in England around 1580 when an 8-year-old boy living near Shrewsbury was rumored to be the result of bestiality between his father and a sheep. The evidence given was that "both his feet were cloven, as was his right hand," and the child, possibly grossly deformed, was taken to be the unquestionable sign of unutterable deviance. Another were-sheep was found at Birdham, near Chichester in 1674, killed by locals and nailed to the church door. It had been placed there so that all churchgoers would see and be reminded of the awful results of bestiality. In the Brocken area of Germany in 1687, according to Johannas Mayer in his *Tuefelbuchen* (published in 1690), a woman was publicly stoned to death for giving birth to a deformed child, which was said to be the consequence of her having sexual congress with a horse. In 1692, another woman in the same region gave birth to a casket of iron nails—one wonders with what *she* had congress? In the same era the English writer Anthony Wood reported seeing the deformed child of an Irishwoman, which he thought had either been "begot by a man but a mastiff dog or a monkey have the semen some sprinkling." Indeed, such ideas continued down until recently, albeit in modified form. The awful deformities of the 19th-century "Elephant Man," John Merrick, were deduced to the fact that his mother had been knocked down and severely frightened by a circus elephant while pregnant with him.

But in both the late-medieval and early modern periods, the gradual notion that physical deformity and transformation were somehow connected with sin—whether sexual or other—was starting to emerge in the public mind. People were transformed, because they were perverse or because they had somehow transgressed God's laws, and their transformation or their monstrous appearance was physical evidence of this. For Christians, those living outside the sphere of Christian teaching and belief were similarly afflicted, and thus portraits of dog-headed Jews and monkey-faced Muslims began to emerge in their literature and art. Those who were excommunicated by the Church ran a similar danger of transformations or of monstrous births.

The Church

The later split within the Church between Catholic and Protestant would lead to further such allegations. It was rumored among Protestants that a number of popes had illegitimate offspring who were born in the shape of beasts—usually wolves. Indeed, so widespread was this belief that in some parts of rural France it was a common saying that the illegitimate son of a priest would almost certainly become a werewolf. It was common Protestant propaganda to claim that many of these terrible offspring—the children of both priests and nuns—were concealed in various remote monasteries and convents all across

Europe. These, argued the Protestant divines, were infallible tokens of the innate corruption and depravity of the Church of Rome, which the Papacy wished to keep secret. In 1579 a pamphlet appeared in England (translated from a French text published in 1523) entitled *Of Two Wonderful Popish Monsters*, which drew attention to the alleged discovery of the body of a pope-ass, which had been found on the banks of the River Tiber in Rome in 1496. This, said the pamphleteer, was incontrovertible evidence of the abhorrence with which God viewed the Catholic Church, in that he should transform the head of the pope—the leader of the Church—into an ass. The other monstrous "wonder" was a monk-calf, which was allegedly born in Freiburg, Germany, on December 8th, 1522. The circumstances of the birth are unclear, but this "monster" may have borne some resemblance to the were-ox that Giraldus described in Wicklow—flattened face, no nose, and large ears. The creature was apparently unable to speak in human tongue, but it was able to ape the monks by making lowing noises like a cow. This was ample evidence of the disdain with which God treated the prayer of Catholic monks and clerics, in that he mocked them with the creature's gibberish. Authorship of this pamphlet was in part ascribed to the Protestant reformer Martin Luther.

The image of the beast-man (and by association the werewolf) was slowly beginning to change. The man who was transformed into a wolf was no longer the kindly creature seeking religious sacraments or doing good—rather, he was now the embodiment of sin and the culmination of vile acts or beliefs. The essential goodness was gone, replaced by a dark and malignant evil. And there was another element that was starting to characterize the werewolf image and that induced abhorrence in all civilized men: cannibalism.

Cannibalism

As societies became more established and centralized, the thought of one man eating another frightened many people. Even today, that same abhorrence is still felt. Although the bible does not specifically ban cannibalism, most developed Western societies tended to consider it as a taboo activity. In fact, there are many references scattered through the Old Testament that seem to actually *promote* it, for example Leviticus 26:29: "And ye shall eat the flesh of your sons; the flesh of your daughters shall ye eat." It was something that the savages did in the wilds beyond the very edges of civilization and it hinted at bestial activity.

Cannibalism, however, may once have been more common in parts of Western Europe than is supposed, and in most cases it conformed to the prejudices of the civilized man. It might have been practiced in the more rural and isolated corners of Europe, and may well have been borne out of necessity in times of famine or during particularly severe winters. For the civilized member of society, however, it was something base and evil, practiced by those who were little more than brute beasts or the agents of the Devil.

Sawney Bean

In early 15th-century Scotland rumors of a particularly atrocious case of cannibalism began to circulate in a number of European countries. This was the story of Sawney Bean, who had been nicknamed the "Maneater of Midlothian." Although today no one is really sure whether Bean and his hideous family actually existed or not, or indeed whether part of the story is an

18th-century invention, it serves to illustrate how cannibalism may have flourished and how certain stories concerning it came to be exploited by succeeding generations. Basically the tale is this:

In the reign of the Scottish king James I (1406–1437), Alexander Bean (also known as Sandy or Sawney Bean), the surly and uneducated son of a hedger and ditcher, set up home in East Lothian with a woman who was as brutish and unlettered as himself. There is no indication as to what trade Bean followed, but it's possible that he made a precarious living as a robber. He is described (admittedly in much later accounts) as brutal, insolent, and overbearing, and his partner seems to have exhibited many of the same qualities. The unsavory pair set up home in a deep cave at Bennane Head near Ballantrae, which was then part of Galloway (today it is part of Ayrshire), where they would live for the next 25 years, keeping very much to themselves and making little contact with the nearby villages. So reclusive were they that few actually knew of their existence. During this time, they maintained themselves by ambushing, robbing, and killing travelers on a nearby moor, taking their bodies back to the cave and cooking and eating them.

It is said that when the authorities did eventually enter the cavern, they found it "like a butcher's kitchen." Deep in the darkness of the cave, Sawney and his partner raised a brood of children—some of whom were feeble-minded and others who were badly deformed—all of whom had the same appetite for human flesh. Many of these children, it was later deposed, had been "begotten in incest," and there is no reason to suppose that this was not the case. And as the family increased, so did the murders of passersby in order to feed them. Indeed, the unexplained disappearances had now reached such a level that the authorities around Ballantrae became seriously worried. They organized a hunt of the immediate area where some of the disappearances had occurred, but because the entrance to Sawney Bean's lair was so well concealed they found nothing. Word soon reached the ears of King James, who decided that the matter should be investigated. By now, bits and pieces of human flesh were washing up a little farther along the coast, as the Beans began to discard fragments of their appalling diet. Limbs were found on a local beach, and to the horror of those who found them some of them seemed to have been gnawed by human teeth. On hearing this, the King took charge of the investigation and began another search of the coast and moor close to Ballantrae. He had heard rumors of an odd hermit who lived with his wife in the vicinity, and thought that there might be some connection with the disappearances.

At the same time they had a piece of luck—a traveler between Ballantrae and Girvan had been attacked by a group of "savages" who had tried to kill him, but he had managed to escape them and raise the alarm. They had fled off across the moors toward the coast. This was the lead the King was looking for, and the hunt began in earnest. The hounds soon found the entrance to the cave, but even they recoiled from the horrors deep inside. It was said that the King was violently sick at the quantities of human remains that were stored there, some of them half-eaten. There were piles of clothes, wallets, money, and valuables, which the cannibals had also stored away without actually realizing the value of what they held.

The clan had spread out through a small cave system, and there seemed to be great numbers of them—according to one account, 48 of them were arrested. In the cool interior caves, human remains were found strung up on meat hooks, as if in a shop. In fact, cannibalism was so ingrained into the Beans' lifestyle that they failed to realize that they had committed any crime. However, the King deemed that they had committed the most abominable acts, and they were taken back as prisoners to the Tollbooth in Edinburgh. From there they were taken to Leith where they were tried and sentenced to death, still wondering what sort of crime they had committed. So gruesome was their crime that the Scottish people took full measure of vengeance upon them. The men were sentenced to have all their limbs amputated and bleed to death, and the women were to be killed in as slow a manner as possible, so that they should suffer every minute. Their bodies were later burned on three separate fires.

One of Sawney's daughters, according to legend, managed to escape the family melee and went to Girvan where she married. She kept her identity and family a secret, becoming a fairly prominent woman in the town. She even planted a local landmark—the "Hairy Tree"—in what was once old Dalrymple Street in the town. However, following the arrest of her father and siblings, her identity did not remain secret for long, and she was seized by an angry and frightened populace. As a sign of public abhorrence at her entire clan, she was hanged from one of the branches of the very tree that she had planted, and her body was subsequently burned. Today, the district of Girvan where she once lived is long gone, and no trace remains of the Hairy Tree.

The tale of Sawney Bean continued to circulate, mainly in England, in the form of pamphlets and articles. It received great notoriety when it appeared in the form of a hack novel (a "penny dreadful" common in the early to mid-1800s) by the jobbing writer Thomas Peckett (or Peskett) Prest (c. 1810–1859) entitled *Sawney Bean: The Man-Eater of Midlothian*, which detailed in gory splendor all the alleged crimes of the Scottish cannibal family. The book brought Bean's name to the fore again and reinforced English prejudices regarding the Scots. Sawney became a byword for vile and unacceptable behavior, and his accounts of his supposed cannibalism shocked civilized English society to its core. There was no doubt in many English minds that there were cannibals north of the border, as exemplified by Sawney Bean.

The story of Sawney Bean began circulating as a "true account" in a number of 17th- and 18th-century English pamphlets and chapbooks around London—the most famous perhaps being *The History of Sawney Beane and His Family: Robbers and Murderers*, which bears no date but is undoubtedly 18th century. Many of these accounts were to be subsequently found within the *Newgate Calendar*, which was compiled around the early 1770s where they were treated as fact. Nevertheless, for such a celebrated case, there is no record of the trial in Pitcairn's *Criminal Trials in Scotland 1494–1624*, which is still regarded as the textbook of historical Scottish jurisprudence. William Roughead wished to include the case in his *Notable British Trials* (1933), but could find no trace of it (although he did write a speculative piece in *Juridical Review* Number 48 the same year).

This has led certain scholars to question whether Sawney Bean actually existed or not. In fact, some have come to the conclusion that the tale was no more than a piece of English propaganda circulated after the defeat of the Jacobites at the Battle of Culloden Moor in 1745. In an attempt to justify the enormous expense of maintaining a victorious English army in Scotland, the authorities sought to portray the Scots as "monsters" sorely in need of "civilizing" (as they had done with the Irish about a hundred years before). The idea of man-eating Scottish monsters, devouring each other in the remoter parts of the country, shocked the English mind and fed them this idea. The English populace were therefore prepared to financially support the occupying English army without much complaint.

Whether or not Sawney Bean actually existed in the form that was claimed by these tales, cannibalism was probably not unknown in the Scottish Highlands. Indeed, it might well have been practiced in some of the more remote villages in the west of the country, and it was on such rumored stories that the propagandists fastened, perhaps shaping some of them into the quasi-mythical figure of Sawney Bean. Many clachans (small villages) on the Highland moors were very remote, and were liable to be cut off in bad weather. When winter took hold and the hunting was poor (many of these places lived on a subsistence level), starvation may have been rife. It was then that cannibalism might have flourished. Old people in the community may have succumbed to the bitter weather, and rather than being buried in the hard ground, could have finished up in the communal stockpot of a famished hamlet.

The Church

The Church took a stance that seemed to suggest that those living in the remoter parts of Scotland were cannibals. Priests and ministers sometimes openly preached that the Scots often ate each other in bleak times. They pointed to the early utterances of St. Jerome (who had experience with the Gauls in the fourth century) in this respect: "Cum ipsi adolestcentus in Gallia viderum Attecottos, gentium Brittanium, humnanis vesci carnibus, et per cum sylvas porocorum geges et armetorum pecudumquerent pasterum nates et feminardum papillas solene abscindere et has solas cibirnum delicias arbetrari." ("He draws attention to the Attecotti, a people of the county now called Scotland, when hunting in the woods preferred the shepherd to his flock and chose only the most delicate and fleshy parts for eating.") Even a small number of Protestant preachers (who shunned Jerome's words as too Catholic) referred in certain sermons to the savagery, brutishness, and cannibalism of the Scots during the aftermath of the English Civil War. However, this may have been propaganda, because the new English Puritan Commonwealth feared an invasion by forces from Presbyterian Scotland, due to broken promises

between the two countries. But the claims may have had some root in reality. The Scottish chronicler and historian Robert Lindsay of Piscottie (1532–1580) relates a tale of a family living "in the wilds" near Oban during the time of James II of Scotland (1437–1460), who were arrested for eating small children who ventured too close to their domain. Most of them were taken to trial in Edinburgh and were subsequently condemned to burning. Their defense would appear to have been that there was no game for them to hunt, so they took and ate the children (and others) as "fair meat." Before the execution, a girl managed to escape, but was recaptured after several days; she was burnt separately. On her way to her death, she leaned from the execution cart and chided some of the crowd who had come to taunt her. She told them that if they knew how sweet the flesh of human children tasted they would want to eat it too. The girl's comments were often repeated with horror and disdain both by politicians and priests alike as a condemnation of the Scots. The story may simply be another variant of the Sawney Bean tale, but it serves to illustrate how the idea of cannibalism was viewed beyond the Scottish borders by the English and the utter abhorrence with which it was regarded by the majority of society.

English and Other Views

Sawney Bean was not the only cannibal to be associated with Scotland. The idea of a bogeyman living just across the Scottish borders held something of a fascination for the English mind. Taking their lead from the monk Andrew of Wyntoun (1350–1423) when he described "Christie o' the Cleek" or "Chweston Cleek," a notorious gang leader whose followers often ate those whom they robbed, many writers referred to an "Andrew Christie," who had attacked English travelers along the Scottish borders. His dates were given as being anywhere in the 14th century (specifically around 1320—before Sawney Bean) up until the 18th century. And there was the actual historical figure of James Douglas, the third Marquis of Queensbury (1697–1715), who was "violently insane" and had to be kept under lock and key at Holyrood in Edinburgh, where he killed, roasted, and ate various servants before his death. Such specters were brought out and waved in English society from time to time in order to shame the Scots.

The English had, of course, no reason to be arrogant or self-righteous in condemning their Scottish neighbors. Although perhaps not as widely reported as their Scottish counterparts, there were instances of cannibalism across the remote parts of the English countryside as well. In parts of the Yorkshire Moors or in the East Anglian Fens there were frequent rumours of cannibalism among the isolated communities there during periods of harsh weather. During the Black Death in the 1350s, for example, when many villages were devastated by plague, there are accounts of starving inhabitants resorting to eating the diseased human flesh of those who were dead or dying in an effort to stay alive. A similar scenario may well have occurred in times of famine or poor harvests.

In more recent times there were hints of cannibalism in Ireland during the Great Potato Famine (1845–1852) when most of the Irish population was at the point of starvation. In places where the Famine hit particularly hard—Counties Clare and Galway—the entire potato crop failed and people in many scattered communities found themselves with nothing to eat. Some ate from the hedgerows, some ate grass like wild beasts, but there are stories still in circulation that some members of the community ate each other. Once again it was the old and the weak that were devoured—those suffering from a "famine fever" (the sickness that often came with the Famine)—and who were less able to defend themselves from the ravages of their starving neighbors. Although no records of local atrocities survive, there is little doubt that such things occurred in certain parts of Ireland, even in the 19th century.

In America too, certain Indian tribes supposedly practiced cannibalism before the coming of the white settlers, although opinion on this is sharply divided. Certainly among some of the Aztec peoples, cannibalism was sanctioned, but there is little evidence that it was ever practiced. There are certainly numerous accounts of some of the Spanish Conquistadors regarding human sacrifice called out by early civilizations, but only scant references to actually eating flesh. Later, it has been said that the ancient Mohawks (upstate New York) ate their enemies. This was alleged by the Algonquin, who continually warred with them; indeed, the Algonquin word for the Mohawk was "one who eats flesh." The ancient Anasazi (the forerunners of the Pueblo Indians of the Southwest) supposedly also practiced cannibalism as part of their rituals during the prehispanic period—although several anthropologists and historians have denied this, pointing out that there is little evidence for such claims. Generally, however, the actual verifiable instances of cannibalism among the Native American tribes is relatively small.

In the slave communities of the Southern States there were whispers and rumors of cannibalism—though once again, these are largely unsubstantiated. In southern Louisiana, for example, there were believed to be colonies of escaped slaves who had fled into the bayou regions and who practiced cannibalism against whites who wandered into their domain. There were whispers of a group of former African slaves calling itself *Le Cochon Gris* who lived deep in the swamp and who practiced cannibalism as part of Voodoo rituals.

However, no substantive evidence for such a cult has ever been found, and its supposed existence owes more to legend than anything else. Nevertheless, such a legend was persistent in places such as New Orleans, and in many respects it was widely believed that such a cult existed somewhere deep in the forests and swamplands of the hinterland, and that it carried out abominable rituals.

There were two slightly more substantial accounts regarding the eating of human flesh among the scattered white communities. Fragmented stories from remote Appalachian villages concerned cannibalism when snows came and meat was scarce. Explorers lost in some of the mountain regions reputedly ate each other as they tried to find their way back to civilization. Perhaps the most famous of all the instances of "white cannibalism" was that which befell the Reed-Donner Wagon Train in the winter of 1846. Subsequent accounts of the catastrophe state no evidences of cannibalism, but initial stories seem to suggest that the eating of human flesh did take place.

The Donners

During 1845 and 1846, pioneers from the East and Midwest were traveling westward to stake out claims for themselves in California, which still lay largely under Mexican control. On April 12, 1846, three farmers from Springfield, Illinois—James Reed and George and Jacob Donner—decided to join them and formed a wagon train of some 87 men, women, and children to head for California. On May 12, the train passed through Independence, Missouri, following a route that had been laid down by previous pioneers. The trail depended on speed, because the final leg of the tail crossed the Sierra Nevada Mountains and the wagons had to reach the high passes before the snows arrived. In Independence, the Donner-Reed Train joined another headed by Captain William H. Russell, and traveled with them along the California

Trail to the Little Sandy River in Wyoming territory. There they camped with a number of others who were heading west, and they discussed shorter ways to reach their goal. One of these was the so-called "Hastings Cut-Off," named after a pioneer named Lansford Hastings. Indeed, it had been Hastings's book *The Emigrant's Guide to Oregon and California* that had encouraged Reed and the Donners to travel west. The Reed-Donner group decided to take the cut-off, which, according to Hastings, would cut anywhere between 150 and 500 miles of their journey (although he was a little vague about the distance). They elected George Donner as their leader; his trail took them across the Wasash Mountains and the Great Salt Lake Desert, rejoining the emigrant trail near present-day Elko, Nevada.

The trail proved more difficult than they had thought—they had to cut through cottonwood thickets and were held up in the Salt Desert (part of present day Utah) and did not rejoin the California Trail until September 26, a full three weeks after the estimated time. There were further difficulties at the Humbolt River in Nevada, which was flooded at the time. Illness and low rations devastated the wagon train as it moved toward the high Sierras; they were, however, too late. As they crossed the mountains, snowstorms hit and the train lost its way in the high passes. Exhausted and low on provisions, the group reached Truckee Lake high in the freezing mountains. Here, three-quarters of them camped (the place is now known as Lake Donner, as the Donners camped out in the nearby Alder Creek Valley. As blizzards set in, 15 of them (10 men and five women) decided to set out and seek help at Sutter's Fort on the western side of the mountains, more than 100 miles away. They set out on snowshoes across the mountains, but as the blizzards hit once more, they soon got lost and wandered through the seemingly endless mountain passes. One of the men fell behind and was swallowed up by the storm, but the others kept on. Eventually food ran out and, starving, they fell on themselves, killing several and cooking them over a rough wood fire. They pressed onward but some had now developed a taste for human meat and several more were killed on the way. Close to death, seven of the expedition (two men and all five women) arrived at Sutter's Fort during a brief lull in the blizzards on January 18, 1847.

Help arrived at Truckee Lake and Alder Creek in four reliefs—the first on February 22, which took 21 refugees. When the second relief arrived, just more than a week later, they found to their horror that the survivors were already beginning to eat the dead and dying. The last of the survivors arrived back in Sutter's Fort on April 29, 1847. Of the 87 emigrants who had set out, more than half were dead, and a number of those had been eaten by their companions. The story of the Reed-Donner wagon train began to circulate throughout America, and was published using sensationalist styles in newspapers and books in a number of towns and cities. The fear of the white cannibal—the person who could eat his or her neighbors—was rising in the popular mind.

All these elements—the thinking wolf, the deformed births that emerged out of sin, and cannibalism—all combined to create the idea of a ravening beast-man, lurking somewhere close by in the common consciousness. This formed the basis for the figure of the werewolf, waiting undetected somewhere in the midst of a community to strike at its fellows. Although this was possibly a common perception in the West, it was France in particular in which such a belief firmly took hold of both society and the law, and it is to this country that we now turn.

4
The French Connection

...They have made bastards of their first origin, this divine form, and transforming themselves into such an impure, cruel and savage beast.

—Beauvais de Chauvincourt, *Discourse de la Lycanthropie*

enri Boguet, senior judge (of Doler) wrote, "There is much disputing." In his *Discours execrable des sorciers* in 1610, he wrote "as to whether it is possible for men to be changed into beasts, some affirming the possibility, whilst others deny it; and there are ample grounds for both views." And though there were arguments among French scholars, theologians, and demonologists as to whether or not such transformations actually occurred, the specter of the wolf and the unfettered beast-man still lurked somewhere deep in the French consciousness.

The Beginning

The notion of werewolves coupled with savagery had arguably preyed on the French mind ever since the Massacre of the Innocents on St. Bartholomew's Day (1572) and the War of the Three Henrys or the Wars of Religion (1584–1598). In the former, the French authorities aided by French Catholics had descended "like wolves" on the numbers of Huguenots (French Protestants) who had gathered in Paris to celebrate the marriage of the Protestant Henry of Navarre (later King Henry IV) to Margaret of Valon. The slaughter had been supposedly engineered by Catherine de Medici, head of the Catholic machinery of government and mother of the weak-willed French monarch, Charles IX. It was said that she unleashed the army with orders to kill as many French Protestants as they could. It is said that the army, aided by the overwhelmingly Catholic populace of Paris, behaved like beasts, tearing the Protestant revellers apart in their frenzy. Following the death of Charles IX, the wars between his younger brother Henry III, the head of the Catholic League Henry de Guise, and the Protestant Henry of Navarre, was an even greater slaughter, with thousands of dead bodies left to rot, and famine and pestilence stalking the land. Faced with this, the wolves slunk from the forests in order to feast. It seemed as though there were wolves everywhere. The canine specter stalked the French mind even after the wars were over.

Peter Stubbe

In 1590 a pamphlet appeared in many parts of France that reinforced such fears. Although the central figure of this publication was not French, but

German, the detail within it ignited many of the terrors that were circulating. The pamphlet was entitled *A True Discourse Declaring the Damnable Life and Death of One Stubbe Peter*, and it was published anonymously. It referred to a certain inhabitant of the German city of Cologne named Peter Stubbe or Stumpf described as being "strong and mighty," with eyes great and large so that in the night they sparkled like brands of fire; a mouth great and wide, with the most sharp and cruel teeth; a huge body; and great paws. In this form, he was as a ravening wolf into which he would transform by wearing an enchanted belt that he had allegedly received from the Devil. When he took it off, he would revert to the proportions of a more normal man "as if he had never been changed." When in an altered shape—many said that it was that of a wolf—Stubbe would become incredibly ferocious, attacking a number of people who crossed his path and then escaping into the surrounding wooded countryside, easily outdistancing hounds that were sent after him. According to some accounts, his first choice of prey was human beings, but if he could not find these, he would attack livestock such as sheep and cattle. He was said to have killed no less than 13 small children and two pregnant women, ripping their unborn babies from their wombs as he ate them. There was no way in which the utter horror of his crimes might be overemphasized. In addition to these vicious crimes, he was further accused of indulging in incest—"like a brute beast"—with his sister and his daughter. He was also accused of killing his son while in his more human form, and of devouring his brains to satisfy "his greedy appetite."

In wolf form, Stubbe was cornered by some hounds on the edge of a field near the village of Bedbur. In order to confuse them, he removed his magic belt and appeared to them as an ordinary man, walking toward the village and leaning on a staff. However, those who had been following the hounds had never taken their eyes off of the wolf, and witnessed the transformation, which they ascribed to the blackest witchcraft. Stubbe was arrested, and under the most terrible torture, he gave a full account of his damnable life. The magic belt was, however, never found—Stubbe claimed that he had abandoned it in "a certain valley" before he was finally captured. However, when the place that he had described was thoroughly searched, no trace of it was found, and so it was assumed that the Devil (in whose service the vicious Stubbe was supposed to be) had reclaimed it as his own. Stubbe's case had now become so celebrated that he could not escape the full rigor of the law. New forms of printing had added to the circulation of the tale, and so accounts of his crimes were read widely all through Germany and also in other countries such as France. His punishment, described in detail in the pamphlet, would make some of his alleged crimes seem rather genteel. He was placed on a great revolving wheel where portions of his flesh were torn away with red-hot instruments, his arms and legs were broken with a wooden axe, he was decapitated, and his body was burnt on a public pyre, along with one of his daughters and a mistress, both of whom were allegedly implicated in his evil deeds. Following the execution, a rather curious monument was set up in Bedbur, consisting of a long pole on which the execution wheel had been placed with a carved image of a wolf on it. At the very top, Stubbe's head had also been mounted as a grisly warning to others not to follow him in making deals with the Devil and adopting the guise of a wolf.

Whether or not Stubbe was able to fully adopt the guise of a wolf or of a man-wolf is uncertain (although the literature seems to suggest the former), but the pamphlet about him was certainly able to inflame the fears of the werewolf or the beast man all across parts of Europe. The horrific details gripped the public imagination and fed into alarmist stories of murderous wolf-like attacks, which were already current within French society.

Gilles Garnier

One of these was the tale of Gilles Garnier, the "hermit of St. Bonnot." During the 1570s, he was living with his wife in a cabin deep in the wooded countryside of Armanges, near the town of Dole. He was not a native of the area, supposedly having come from Lyons, and was considered to be odd and extremely belligerent in his ways. Around the time that he had come to love Armanges, a large and ferocious wolf began to prey on the flocks of local shepherds, spreading fear and alarm throughout the district. In addition, the creature carried off several small children into the surrounding forests and a number of witnesses claimed that these innocents were the victims of a werewolf. The story spread, and a fear of some supernatural being dwelling in the woodlands began to grow steadily. Naturally, local suspicions fell on the queer hermit dwelling there, and though these were frequently voiced, the authorities still hadn't enough evidence to confront him. As the alarm grew, the local parliament (governing body) decided to take some action. It issued a proclamation calling on all able-bodied men armed with pikes, arquebuses, sticks, and halberds to assemble and to hunt down the werewolf. This vigilante group soon began its task and was quickly able to hunt down its prey. A little girl was rescued from the jaws of a wolf in La Poupee meadow, between Authune and Chastenoy. She had been badly mauled by the animal, but as her rescuers drove it off, they were allegedly shocked to notice an uncanny resemblance between the muzzle of the beast and the face of the misanthropic hermit of St. Bonnot. This was the evidence they needed, and the parlement in Dole issued that Garnier be arrested and questioned in connection with the attack.

The hermit seems to have been slow-witted and gave rambling excuses and explanations, but when "put to the question" (most probably tortured), he admitted that he was indeed a werewolf. He was brought to trial at the very beginning of 1573 under the public prosecutor, Henri Camus. He was found guilty and executed on January 18.

He gave pleaded guilty and had given long and gruesomely detailed accounts of his time as a werewolf. The central part of his confession concerned the murder of two small boys, ages 10 and 12, one of whom he had killed in the vicinity of Dole and the other (in August 1570) in a pear orchard near the village of Perrouze in the parish of Cromany. As he had been devouring the latter, he had been driven off, still in his wolf form, by the approach of some laborers. In that same October, he had killed a small girl who had been playing in a wood called La Serre, about a mile or so from Dole, saying that he found her flesh "especially sweet." On returning to human form, he took some of it home in order to cook it for his evening meal.

Unlike Peter Stubbe, Garnier was extremely vague as to how he actually transformed himself into a wolf. There was no magic belt or alleged contact with the Devil. Instead, Garnier simply said that he became a wolf through "sorcery," although it is unclear how he achieved this and what methods he used. In some accounts, he claimed to have met with a phantom or "spectral man" deep in the woods of St. Bonnot, who had taught him various magical arts including transformation. In another account Garnier says that he simply heard a voice "between the trees" instructing him what to do. Interestingly, he also speaks of "strangling" his victims. Could it be that the weak-minded and confused Garnier simply *imagined* himself to be a wolf in order to commit his dastardly murders? Could his offence be actually one of cannibalism rather than werewolfery? Of course, this statement throws out the evidence of those who saw him as a wolf, because they claimed similarities between the feral wolf and the man; could they too have been mistaken? Perhaps the poorly educated and wretched Garnier and his wife gave in to unnatural urges in order to survive in the depths of the forest? Or could it have been a conspiracy simply to get rid of the odd and antisocial hermit? Such social or mental niceties were not taken into account by the officials in Dole, who were required to carry out the trial and execution of the sullen Garnier.

Following his trial, they refused to offer him the mercy of strangulation before his body was completely burned—it was a harsh punishment and one that was supposedly designed to reflect the terrible crimes he was alleged to have committed. The harshness of the sentence may also have reflected the continuing fear civilized Frenchmen had for the supposed feral beast, which might be lurking in the heart of their communities.

The Three Werewolves

Indeed, the Garnier case stirred echoes of another alleged werewolf trial a little while earlier. And this time, there was more than one beast. Around 1520, three werewolves were reputedly found living near the village of Poligny in the Jura region near the Swiss Alps. This was a remote and mountainous area, thickly forested and full of wild tales of the loup-garou, an evil spirit closely identified with the Devil, who went about doing mischief in the form of a giant mastiff dog. The first of these wolf-men to be discovered was Michael Verdung (also known as Michael Udon), who had allegedly been wounded by a traveler whom he had attacked. Following a marked trail of blood, several local men found their way to his cabin where they saw a woman tending to his bleeding wounds. The matter was put in front of the Inquisitor General at Besancon, who began a thorough investigation into the incident, including "questioning" Verdung himself. Under torture, he implicated another man—Pierre Bourgot, known locally as Big Peter.

This man was widely known for his surly temperament, his irascible temper, and his odd ways, and so it came as no surprise to his neighbors that he might be associated with such a supernatural crime as werewolfery. Placed under torture himself, Big Peter admitted to being a werewolf and described how this had come about. While out hunting for some sheep, which had been scattered during a storm, he was approached by three dark horsemen to whom he told his troubles. One of them promised Bourgot peace and contentment if he would take the three as his masters and do whatever they asked. Bourgot promptly agreed, and very shortly after, he found his lost sheep. A few days later, the three horsemen appeared at his house, and the one who had spoken to him now revealed himself as an instrument of the Devil. He made Big Peter renounce his Christian faith and swear allegiance to the Evil One by kissing his left hand. Later Bourgot regretted what he'd done—he was now in thrall to Satan after all—but just as he was going to go to the priest and confess what he'd done, Michael Verdung appeared at his door. Verdung claimed to be an agent of the Devil and promised him gold and wealth if he would not inform the priest and if he would renew his oath to the Evil One. He made Peter disrobe and smeared him with some sort of magic ointment, which transformed him into the guise of a wolf. In this form, Verdung informed him, they could go the Devil's Sabbat—a great gathering of witches, which the Devil himself would attend—and they could be restored to their human shapes by another special ointment which he (Verdung) had in his possession.

When in wolf form, Bourgot experienced fearful lusts and desires that he couldn't control, including the desire to eat human flesh—especially that of children. He had, for example, eaten the flesh of a four-year old child whom he had mauled; he found it especially sweet and delicious. He had also broken the neck of a nine-year-old girl and devoured her as well. Michael Verdung had also assumed a wolf shape and had accompanied him on his terrifying expeditions—not only this, but they had both copulated with various female wolves that they had met in the forest. Faced with such a catalogue of horror and perversion, the authorities felt that they had no other option but to execute them both and burn their bodies.

As stories of Giles Garnier and the werewolves of Poligny began to circulate throughout France, the notion of the man-beast began to become more firmly established in the popular mind. People began to panic and to see werewolves everywhere. The unsettled and hostile mood of the times often contributed to an overall atmosphere of suspicion and mistrust. Strangers were viewed with alarm, particularly if their ways were unfamiliar and strange. The case of Jacques Roulet illustrates such tension.

Jacques Roulet

In 1598, a soldier was walking through some fields near Angiers in the French northwest along with some local peasants, when he came across a wild-looking half-naked beggar crouching among some bushes. There were scratches and blood across his hands and face, and, on pulling him out, the group found that there were pieces of what looked like human flesh under his long and ragged fingernails. On searching further through the undergrowth, they found the body of a 15-year-old boy.

The beggar's name was Jacques Roulet, and he was both mentally retarded and epileptic. Although there was actually no direct evidence to emphatically connect him to the murder, he was taken in for questioning and thrown into prison in Angiers. It is not formally recorded as to whether he was questioned (although he may have been tortured), but at some point he gave a full admission and account of werewolfery. He was brought before the local magistrate—Judge Pierre Herault—where he admitted that he had a magic ointment. If he rubbed the ointment into his skin he would change into the guise of a wolf. Judge Herault, who was somewhat skeptical of the account given the prisoner's obvious mental condition, asked him if he *dressed* as a wolf, but Roulet denied this, saying that he took the body of the actual animal with great, rending paws. He was unclear, however, about the appearance of his head, and thought that he might have retained a human countenance whilst having the body of the wolf. In his lupine form, he attended a number of Devil's Sabbats, which were also frequented by several others of his kind.

There is no record of what exactly happened to Jacques Roulet after his trial, but it is likely that he was found guilty, executed, and burned. It is thought that the court considered his confession to be so abominable that it ordered the documents concerning it to be burnt, and so only fragments of the case survive.

The Tailor of Chalons

The year 1598 seems to have been a notable time for werewolves and a period when the beast-men were particularly troublesome. One of the most notable and widely publicized came from the town of Chalons in the Champagne region where a local tailor supposedly committed cannibalistic crimes. He allegedly attacked several children playing near his shop, which lay just within the town boundary, taking their bodies away to the nearby woods and fields where he reputedly ate their flesh like a wolf. He then stored their bones among some chests and barrels at the back of his premises. When these were accidentally discovered, his horrid crimes were exposed, and he was dragged away to the prison in Chalons, accused of being a werewolf. What became of him is unknown, but it is likely, similar to Jacques Roulet, that he was burned—although this cannot actually be confirmed, as the directives of the court appear to have been destroyed. There is also no record to state if the tailor was actually (or believed himself to be) transformed into a wolf or whether these were merely cannibal crimes. No matter what form they took, they were inevitably associated with the notion of the beast-man.

Werewolf Hysteria
The Gandillions

Lycanthropes were now coming very much to the fore in the French mind, and werewolf hysteria seemed to be gradually growing. In the Franche-Comte region, near the Swiss Alps, not far from Poligny where Michael Verdung and Pierre Bourgot had been arrested, a whole *family* of werewolves was discovered. The area was very remote and almost inaccessible, thickly forested and extremely mountainous. In the spring of 1598 two children were fruit-picking near the village of St. Claude in Burgundy when 16-year-old Bonoit Bidel momentarily left his sister at the foot of a tree as he climbed into the branches to pick more fruit. As he was climbing, tragedy struck. A "tail-less" wolf suddenly emerged from the nearby forest and attacked the defenseless girl. Bonoit, who was armed with a sharp knife that he'd been using for cutting down fruit, immediately jumped to the ground to defend his sister. The wolf, however, seemed to change in front of him, becoming something like a beast-man with a human face and fur-covered hands. It struck the knife away and delivered the boy a fatal blow on the neck. The girl screamed, alerting some peasants working in a nearby field, who came and drove the "wolf" away. Benoit was close to death, but he was still able to give them information concerning the "wolf" creature, and, after arming themselves, they mounted a search of the surrounding countryside. In some woods close by, they found a girl named Perenette Gandillion wandering among the trees. She had scratches on her face and traces of blood on her dress, and in a mixture of outrage and fear, the mob tore her to pieces.

The Gandillions lived close by and everyone now began to take a closer interest in their activities. They had long been suspected of being witches and Devil-worshippers—they were viewed as a reclusive and largely antisocial family—and the authorities now had an excuse to investigate further. Other members of the family were arrested and put on trial. Perenette's sister, Antoinette, was accused of being a werewolf and creating hailstorms by way of dark magic. She was also accused of venturing up into the mountains to attend a witch's Sabbat, and of copulating with the Devil in the form of a great man-goat.

Her brother, Pierre Gandillion, was similarly accused. The boy was subject to swoons and epileptic fits, and was said to lie at home in a supposed coma, as his spirit roamed the countryside in the form of a wolf, doing harm to all that it met. He was also accused of attending the Devil's Sabbat and of taking part in a huge gathering comprised entirely of werewolves. Under torture, he revealed how Satan had given him and others clothes made of wolf skin, and had made him run about the countryside on all fours attacking animals and humans in order to satisfy unholy appetites. Pierre's son, Georges, also confessed to having a magic salve that would transform him into a wolf. Together with Perenette and Antoinette he attacked and killed a neighbor's goat while under the spell of the salve.

A new and slightly more sinister figure began to emerge in the St. Claude case. This was the Grand Justice of the Franche-Comte region, Henri Boguet (1550–1619), a University-educated lawyer who had made a special study of witchcraft and demonology cases. His book on the subject, which circulated throughout France and beyond, was entitled *Discours des sorciers*, and was an exhaustive (if utterly biased) text, which became a staple for French witch-hunters and magistrates long after his death in 1619. Witches and creatures of darkness, he said, were everywhere, and the authorities must be vigilant. He pointed to his own record of trying and executing more than 600 sorcerers in the Franche-Comte and Jura regions alone between 1598 and 1616. He was also especially adept at finding instances of witchcraft and diabolic practice amongst the Jews of the area. When the St. Claude cases broke, his book on witchcraft was already in print, and he was already regarded as France's leading demonologist; however, as he began his investigations into the Gandillion family, he decided to release a second edition of the volume, which contained a special and specific chapter on lycanthropy. He declared that anybody who yielded themselves to the Devil might be transformed into ravening beasts, and he used the Gandillion family as an example of such evil practice. He claimed he had observed members of the family walking on all fours around their cells in the "manner of beasts," just as they had in the fields around their home. He also noted that Pierre Gandillion was so disfigured that he actually resembled an animal. All this had developed an appetite for human flesh within the family. Boguet's words were taken extremely seriously, both by the clergy and learned men, and without doubt contributed to the growing French hysteria concerning werewolves dwelling in the midst of ordinary communities.

Having burnt the Gandillions, Boguet now turned his attention to seeking out any other werewolves that might be lurking in the Jura region. Indeed, his efforts against suspected lycanthropes seem to have increased, although it is unclear whether or not he actually found any. However, with throngs of people now being brought before the courts, accusations enabled children such as the Gandillions to extract a confession. His most famous book on the subject *La Demonomanie des Sorciers* (translated into English as *On Witchcraft*), stated that the Devil took many forms, all of which were interchangeable, even between human and animals, and that those who had the powers to take on such shapes were living among God's children and must be rooted out. This was the function of the witch-hunter, and it legitimized the horrors that local French magistrates put many alleged witches through.

Pierre de Rostegny

One such magistrate was Pierre de Rostegny (also known as Pierre de Lancre, 1553–1631), a judge in Bordeaux who conducted a ferocious witch-persecution in the Labourd area of Brittany in 1609. This area comprised mainly Basques, a people for whom the prejudiced de Lancre had the utmost contempt and hatred, considering them to be superstitious and irreligious. As a magistrate he commenced a program of persecution against them, burning more than 700 of them at the stake around 1609 and 1610. Basque women, he believed, were little more than libertines, and Basque men were only slightly above the level of the brute beast. Similar to other magistrates, he produced a widely circulated book, *Tableau de l'inconstance des mauvais Anges et Demons* (published in 1613), which further strengthened the impression of witches and other evil creatures living at the very heart of local communities and the idea that individuals might transform themselves into the guise of animals.

Faced with a plethora of texts on witchcraft and diabolism, the French populace was now on the edge of hysteria regarding evil creatures within their midst. Beast-men lurked everywhere, and anyone who acted oddly or suspiciously might well be in league with the Evil One. The unsettled atmosphere of the times with Protestant versus Catholic and authorities trying to reassert some form of control over the situation, however biased and haphazard that was, only inflamed the situation. Matters were quickly reaching a head.

Jean Grenier

The matter that is generally regarded as bringing a culmination to the French werewolf trials in 1603 was that of Jean Grenier. Grenier, the son of a poor laborer in the village of St. Antoine de Pizon, a district under the Lower Court of St. Sevier of the Parliament of Bordeaux, is generally regarded as one of the last French lycanthropes. The magistrate in the case was Pierre de Lancre. At the time of the trial, he had increased his jurisdiction in pursuit of the Basques, and now extended his authority beyond French borders and into part of Spain.

Jean Grenier was an odd 14-year-old boy who probably had mental problems; he liked to frighten local girls and small children with the claim that he was a werewolf. And, as time went on, his assertions grew wilder and wilder. He claimed he had been approached by the Devil in the form of a mysterious stranger while out in the fields near his home and had been given a magic salve, together with a wolfskin cloak, that would transform him into a wolf for the space of one hour on certain nights of the week. He further claimed to be the illegitimate son of a priest—his accepted father was generally known to not be his real father—and it was a current belief in many parts of France that the sons of priests often became werewolves and would serve the Devil.

When in his wolf shape, Grenier claimed that he had attacked several dogs, but had found their blood disgusting. Sometimes he claimed that he had also killed several young children, and had found that their blood was far sweeter—although he was not terribly specific about those whom he had devoured. Though these were clearly the fantasies of a disturbed adolescent mind, they were taken seriously by his neighbors in the countryside. While out tending sheep one day with 13-year-old Margeruite Porier, he began to tell his wild tales of being a werewolf. Frightened, the girl accused him of turning into a werewolf before her eyes and of attacking her. She claimed Jean had gone off into some trees, and had re-emerged in his wolf form. She had managed to beat the creature off, but it had only retreated a little way, sat on its haunches, and growled at her, ready to spring. She said it looked like Jean Grenier. At this stage, she had run away and managed to escape. She said the beast was smaller than an ordinary wolf and it had no tail—a sure sign among many of the locals that it was a werewolf. Grenier was arrested and brought to court.

Given the severity of the accusations against him, he was expected to deny all charges but, surprisingly he admitted everything, confessing to a number of other instances of werewolfery with an almost obscene relish. Throughout the previous months a number of local children had gone missing and Grenier seemed anxious to connect himself with their disappearances. This element added great importance to his rambling and often disjointed confessions. Acting on some of the accounts he gave, the authorities began to check the details, but found nothing of any consequence—the "confessions" were no more than the fevered imaginings of a disordered mind, and had really no substance to them. Grenier now changed his story a little and began to implicate other people whom he knew and whom he claimed were also werewolves. A number of his neighbors were arrested and imprisoned. A thorough search was made of the Grenier household in order to discover the alleged magic salve, but nothing was found. Jean's father was arrested and tortured, and in the end confessed that he had indeed been a werewolf and had approached several little girls. However, he claimed he never ate them, just "played with them."

Today, this might have led observers to believe that the older man was a pedophile who was attracted to small female children and that his teenage son shared some of these proclivities and fantasies. However, in 17th-century

France, it was taken that both father and son were both supernatural entities. It is possible that pedophilia was well beyond the understanding of the French court and the case was conducted on the grounds of witchcraft and lycanthropy alone. Taking advantage of the situation, a number of young local girls—some of whom had seen their friends actually carried off by wolves—gained limited fame by making allegations of their own against the Grenier family, who were not all that popular and were widely disliked in the district. Jean's father was tortured again, and he implicated his son and recanted the crimes to which he had confessed. Based on what was admittedly the flimsiest of evidence, Jean was brought before the courts in the Coutras in June 1603. With alarming speed the French legal system found him guilty of witchcraft and lycanthropy and sentenced him to be hanged. The case was over, but the law was not yet finished with Jean Grenier.

The following September, the case was reviewed by the Parliament of Bordeaux under the chairmanship of Pierre de Lancre. Again he told his story about becoming a wolf, adding other embellishments and seeking to implicate those who had turned against him and who had offered hostile testimony. He told the court that as an 11-year-old child, he had been taken deep into the woodlands close to his home by one of his neighbors in order to meet a dark man whom he called "le Maitre de Foret" (Master of the Forest).

The Master, who was assumed to be the Devil, scratched him with a long fingernail, leaving a distinct mark, and gave him the magic salve and the wolfskin cloak in order to be able to change shape. He further confessed that while in his wolf form, he had entered a house in a village, the name of which he could not remember, and had dragged a baby from its cradle and devoured it. Shortly after, he encountered a true wolf and shared with it what was left of the child.

Some time after, in the parish of St. Antoine de Pizon, he attacked and killed a young girl in a black dress who was looking after some sheep in a field. The area had now become a favorite hunting ground for him—two months earlier he had attacked and almost completely eaten a small boy who was playing in a large yard, and six weeks earlier he had mauled and devoured yet another small child who was crossing a bridge. He claimed he had fought with several dogs, killing all of them except one in the town of Eparon whose owner had suddenly appeared and had driven him away with a rapier.

Once again he repeated his assertion (which was given with such conviction that it was considered at the time to be true) that his acknowledged father was not his actual father. He declared that he was secretly the son of a priest, and that this was why le Maitre de Foret had approached him and had lured him into evil ways. Later, contradicting himself, he said that his supposed illegitimacy and his priestly connections had given him "special powers," which included being able to turn himself into an animal. No mention was made of the "black man" of the woodlands. However, upon investigation, this was all found to be the total fabrication of a confused mind—his father, a local laborer, was arrested and tortured once more, and acknowledged that Jean was indeed his own child. There had been an extremely difficult relationship between father and son—Jean's natural mother had died and his father had remarried. Jean and his stepmother didn't get on very well, for she found his ways extremely strange and sometimes frightening, and his father had eventually put him out of the house and had reduced him to beggary, forcing him to wander around the countryside seeking food. The boy had tried to get work, but was notoriously unreliable, so few would employ him. He had, however, a rather vivid imagination and, during his travels, he terrorized small children with his lurid tales of werewolfery and Devil-worship.

Relations between him and his father were so sour that it is not surprising that one tried to implicate the other in the whole sordid affair. However, when Jean faced his father in court, his testimony began to break—he faltered, contradicted himself in some of his evidence, and withdrew some of his allegations against the man. He now told the court that his mother had thrown him out, because she had seen him going about on all fours behaving like a dog and vomiting up the fingers of a small child. This had terrified her and she had driven him from the house. He repeated the stories about eating the little girl in the black dress and the boy in the yard. These appear to have been total fantasies, for the court had no records of any such children having disappeared. His father was eventually dismissed without charge.

Despite all these crazy allegations, the review court took Jean Grenier extremely seriously. In many ways, it suited de Lancre's theories of devilry and evil creatures lurking just beneath the surface of a more civilized society in order to tempt God's servants. Thus, the review was recorded in lurid and horrible detail. However, by the beginning of the 17th century, the popular mood in France was starting to change slightly, and this is reflected in the sentence that the review court handed out, which was less severe than that of the lower jurisdiction. It took into account the boy's "stupidity," that he was a beggar and malnourished, and that, bereft of his natural mother, he had been raised by a cruel stepmother who left him to fend for himself without anyone to take an interest in him. Given these circumstances was it any wonder that Jean Grenier appeared as such a pathetic specimen and easy prey for the Devil and his minions? However, he was not beyond salvation. Although he had been sentenced to be hanged and burnt, the senior court now rescinded that punishment and decreed that he should live out the rest of his days as a prisoner in a Christian monastery. Here, it was hoped, he would eventually renounce his evil ways and turn to the true path of Christ. And with that Jean Grenier vanishes from the pages of recorded history.

Bete de Gevaudon

Although the Jean Grenier case is regarded as being one of the last such trials in the country, France had still not finished with its werewolves. The beast that lurked somewhere at the back of the French mind refused to go away. It returned once more in 1764 with the infamous Bete de Gevaudon, high in the Massif Centrale region. Similar to the Jura, this was a remote and mountainous region with scattered communities living among thick forests and woodlands. In the village of Lagogne, in the Gevaudon, a ferocious wolf-like animal suddenly started attacking and killing people who ventured too near the forest edge. The death toll rose swiftly to 11, which included well-known local laborers, and alarm began to spread rapidly throughout the village. Although it is probable that the deaths were caused by a pack of wolves dwelling in the forest, rather than a single animal, it did not take long for the ancient lycanthropic fears of former centuries to re-emerge. Certainly the possibility of a large wolf-pack in the forest was acknowledged, but deep-seated local folklore and folk-wisdom now began to hint at something supernatural—a werewolf living close by. These old tales were aided by a relatively new feature in the area: the printed word. Broadsheets and pamphlets began to circulate widely, recounting old stories and gradually moving the focus toward rumor of lycanthropy. Many of these circulars carried monstrous and diabolic-looking woodcuts and drawings, showing a terrifying and threatening figure—a half-man, half-beast crouching in the shadows of the forest ready to spring on some unsuspecting victim. Such images only served to prey on local fears and raised regional hysteria. These were supported by often garbled accounts of strange bestial figures, half-glimpsed in the forests, particularly in the woods at Mazel-le-Grezes. In one of these reputed accounts, a woman on her way to Mass saw a beast man in the form of a wolf with brass buttons around the throat, as if the wolfskin were an overcoat that had been buttoned over a human form. In another, a woodsman saw a large shaggy shape running along the woodland floor on all fours—it had, he said, the shape of a man. Another woman, also on her way to church, was accosted by a large shaggy man, covered in dark fur, who walked alongside her for part of the way, but who promptly vanished as soon as she screamed the name of Christ. This was a sure sign, she declared, that her companion had either been the Devil or one of his agents. And she was sure that this being had been a werewolf. Soon after, the killings stopped (perhaps the wolf pack moved on) and the Bete de Gevaudon was never caught. The terror, however, lingered on all through the region.

There is little doubt that many of the alleged sightings of wolf-men were no more than the imaginations of local folk spurred on by the re-emergence of old folktales and folk beliefs. They serve to illustrate, however, that although France had moved on since the days of Jean Grenier, and that there was now a more or less formal acknowledgement that werewolves did not exist, there was still an element of uncertainty about the issue, particularly in the rural mind. Folktales and ancient legends concerning those who could transform themselves into beasts or wolves that could speak with a human voice were still pretty much a staple in some parts of the French countryside. Even though the instance of the Bete de Gevaudon was probably the most famous of these tales, there were other stories from other parts of rural France similar in tone and that hinted at werewolves living among the populace.

Little Red Riding Hood

Some of these stories (known as *contes* in France) drew the attention of serious collectors of folktales. The French writer of fairy stories and collector of legends, Charles Perrault, quickly recognized the importance of some of

the old wolf-tales that were still circulating around the end of the 17th century. In 1697, he published a collection of folktales including one that had a werewolf theme about a speaking wolf that could create mayhem. Whether or not this was based on an actual folktale is unclear, but it contained elements that were current in many French werewolf tales of the period. It dealt with a petite fille, a pretty young girl (little more than a child) who had to journey through a dark forest in order to take some groceries to her grandmother who was ill. The

images of the small girl and the dark forest were stock characteristics of many tales concerning werewolves and held echoes of the Jean Grenier case, which at that point was only 80 years old. In order to journey through the cold, dank wood, the little girl put on her favorite garment, a cape of red material.

On her way among the trees, she was approached by a wolf that suddenly emerged from the undergrowth. It engaged her in conversation, questioning her closely about her errand and destination. From her it learned the exact location of her grandmother's house and that the old lady was both ill and housebound. However, it did not attack her due to the presence of some woodsmen nearby. But it too expressed concern for the old lady's well-being and announced that it too would visit her, but suggested that it would take a slightly different path than the little girl. This plan was dressed up as a game, a race to see who would get to the house first. The little girl took the longer path and on the way she became distracted by picking flowers and watching the woodland creatures.

Meanwhile, the wolf had already reached the cottage, and, mimicking the voice of the little girl, it persuaded the old woman to open the door and let it in. Whereupon it leapt on the grandmother in her bed and devoured her. Climbing into bed, it put on the old lady's nightgown and waited for the little girl to arrive. When she did, the wolf pretended to be the bedridden old lady and invited her in. There was some conversation between the two concerning the hugeness of the "grandmother's" eyes, the largeness of her mouth, and the sharpness of her teeth, but in the end, the wolf revealed who it really was, and, leaping on the little girl, completely devoured her. There is no happy ending to this tale. It is, however, not hard to recognize the children's story of *Little Red Riding Hood,* which most of us have read at one time or another, although this version of the tale is known as *Le Grand Mal Garou,* which Perrault collected somewhere in a region of southern France near the Spanish border. It may have its source in the tales of Giles Garnier, the werewolves of Poligny, and Jean Grenier, stretching back for more than a century. The wolf attacks both a little girl and a bedridden old lady, both defenseless victims and both suggestive of the allegations made in several of the werewolf trials. Indeed, it is quite possible that in France, *Little Red Riding Hood* started out as a particularly gruesome werewolf tale. In fact, in another French version of the same story, the little girl first encounters the wolf in its human form and therefore feels no fear. Of course, it is weird that in the fairy tale she does not find a speaking wolf either strange or frightening. Perrault was careful to constantly keep the wolf in its lupine form and not as a hybrid creature, for maximum effect.

The French version (which may be the oldest) ends unhappily with the death of Little Red Riding Hood in the jaws of the wolf. Other variants of the same tale, however, had a much happier outcome. In a German variant, the ending is much more satisfactory from the human perspective. This tale was published in the Brothers Grimm's famous collection of German folktales (mainly for children) *Kinder und Hausmarchen* in 1812. This story is known as *Rotkappchen* or Red Cap, which gives us our more familiar Anglicised title of Red Riding Hood. The German version parallels the French, but only up to a point, for in this narrative the little girl's cries attracted the attention of a passing huntsman or a nearby woodcutter who rushed in to save her. Using a knife or an axe blade, he slit open the wolf's belly and thus freed Red Riding Hood and her grandmother. In a rather confused development of the story, the wolf seemed to be mysteriously asleep throughout this operation, having gorged itself, and so they replaced the escaped victims with a large stone, which the grandmother sewed into the creature's stomach. When the wolf awoke, it attempted to escape, but the weight of the stone dragged it down and killed it.

The German ending was therefore much more satisfactory from a storyteller's standpoint. This more wholesome element was developed and expanded in Britain during Victorian times when many grisly old European folktales were "sanitized" into children's bedtime stories for popular consumption, and it is perhaps one of these versions with which most of us are familiar.

Whether it was based on a genuine folktale or not, the story of Red Riding Hood certainly reflected a number of elements, both explicit and implicit, which were current in old werewolf tales, many of which dated from a time long before Perrault. The color of the girl's cape or cloak is the color of blood, suggestive of a potential victim; she must be very naïve if she is led astray by the wiles of a talking wolf (which takes the place of the role of the Devil), and, of course, there is the notion of a demonic force masquerading firstly in the guise of a human and later in a destructive animal form. All of these images have traditions and associations that stretch well back into prehistoric times.

It has also been suggested that the tale of Red Riding Hood may have political connotations and that it may in fact be an old Huguenot fable. Although there is scant evidence for this, it was allegedly circulated following the St. Bartholomew's Day Massacre in 1572, as a disguised symbol of the brutality and savagery of the French Monarchy—the color red in the little girl's cape symbolizing the color of freedom. Red caps were sometimes worn by Huguenot patriots as a symbol of their independence from Catholicism and from the (largely Catholic-controlled) machinery of State. The idea of the Huguenot movement being swallowed up by the Catholic monarchy and then freed by ripping it asunder, it has been argued, may have formed the inspirational basis for the tale. Although this may be stretching the idea of the werewolf story a bit far, there is little doubt that the shadow of the wolf still lay dormant in some corner of the French consciousness, just waiting to be aroused.

But it was not just Gallic folktales, politically motivated or not, in which the werewolf appeared. The plethora of French trials had attracted interest, not only from those who collected such tales, but among rational thinkers as well. The times were changing and a new mood of scientific enquiry was becoming the norm in much of Europe. Old beliefs and superstitions, which had lain unquestioned for centuries, were now coming under the searchlight of more rigorous investigation. The question now arose: if the likes of Giles Garnier, the werewolves of Poligny, and Jean Grenier were *not* in fact werewolves at all (and the general consensus suggested that they might not be, as is evidenced by the more lenient sentence passed on Grenier by the Senior Court in Bordeaux), then what were they? Several leading physicians took up the case with reference to the French cases.

Medical Concerns

Even in the early 16th century when the trials were getting underway, some voices questioned the underlying notions of witchcraft and werewolfery. One of these early skeptics was a German physician named Dr. Johann Weyer (or Weir, 1515–1588), who suggested that there might be some form of medical or mental condition underlying both the behavior and confessions of some of these unfortunates. Weyer is generally regarded as the first man to use the term "mentally ill" to describe the actions and undoubted fantasies of some of these alleged witches and werewolves. He appears to have been a logical and humane doctor, genuinely seeking some sort of explanation for the supposed condition. Pointing to some of the French werewolf cases (and some of the witch "trials" in his own country), he argued that such people were deluded and the confession of bestial behavior coupled with fantastical stories about meeting the Devil and using magical salves were little more than the outpourings of disturbed minds. Such people, he went on, had only "become animals" in their own minds and were in more need of help than punishment. As the Enlightenment took hold in Europe, others followed Weyer's line of thinking. Mental problems, harsh living conditions, loneliness, and isolation in certain cases all contributed to overall behavioral problems, which might be classed as werewolfery. And indeed, magistrates such as Pierre de Lancre had been forced to realize this in the Jean Grenier case when he commented that the wretchedness of Jean's existence had perhaps contributed in no small measure to his alleged crimes. Beginning with Weyer's direction, and perhaps in some ways as a result of the French trials, the way in which supposed werewolves were viewed was beginning to change. And it is to those changing perspectives that we must now turn our attention.

5

Barking Mad

A very pestilential disease, my lord,

They call it lycanthropia.

—John Webster, *The Duchess of Malfi*

In his celebrated book *De praestigiis daemonum* (The Illusion of Demons, published in 1563), the German physician Dr. Johann Weyer openly attacked the superstition and allegedly false beliefs that had characterized both the witch and werewolf trials of former years. He denounced the *Malleus Mallificarum* written by the inquisitors Sprenger and Kramer, which had become the Church's official handbook in tracking down such creatures. The persecution of confused and mentally vulnerable people was urged, and the authorities began to look upon them with compassion rather than censure.

Dr. Johann Weyer

Weyer was a follower of the Cologne sage Heinrich Cornelius Agrippa von Nettesheim (1486–1535), who acknowledged the prevalence of the dark arts, but had also argued that everything, including occultism, philosophy, and medicine, formed part of an all-embracing and cohesive whole. In his view, the supernatural and rational world might be brought together through diligent enquiry. In this, Weyer's book must be considered as one of the earliest volumes to display an enlightened attitude toward the immanence of the diabolic world, and can be regarded as one of the foundations of a modern psychological approach with regard to alleged witchcraft and shapeshifting.

In his work, he made specific reference to werewolves, drawing on the French werewolf trials for his evidence. Those who had been accused may have suffered from "a disorder of their melancholic humour." He discussed a list of medical symptoms that might make the victims rise from their beds at night and prowl around the countryside imagining that they were wolves or some other sort of beast. Weyer suggested a number of "cures" for such a condition—perhaps by bloodletting to restore the balance of the humors (as Roman physician Galen suggested) or perhaps making them eat fruits to take away their insatiable cravings for meat and so restore their natural senses. Changes of diet and exercise were essential, he argued, to restore the "humeral balance." Weyer specifically considered the case of the Werewolves of Poligny, who had confessed to eating small children and attending diabolic Sabbats with both witches and the Devil while in a wolf form. These people, Weyer suggested, were not actually mentally ill, but were simply deluded.

He was careful not to rule out any direct involvement by the Evil One; indeed, he acknowledged that these people might actually have met with the Devil (although what the term "Devil" meant in Weyer's opinion is open to question). He went on to suggest that the Father of Lies might have befuddled and misguided their brains so much that all sorts of delusions might have set in. They therefore believed a number of things about themselves, none of which were true. Such delusions may well have been compounded by the use of supposed amulets and salves, some of which were made from questionable herbs, and may well have contained hallucinogenic properties, distorting their perceptions and making them imagine things. Thus their minds were confused even further. In many respects Weyer was far ahead of his time and appears to have been one of the earliest physicians to combine a rudimentary strand of psychoanalysis with the possibility of psychotropic drugs. He was also among the first to place the accepted view of lycanthropy (that it was the result of evil doing in a new light).

Reginald Scot

And elsewhere the times and perceptions were also changing. Old and previously unshakeable beliefs were now being openly questioned, and others were now beginning to follow Weyer's example. One of these was an Englishman, a Kentish squire named Reginald Scot (1538–1599). A former Justice of the Peace, he had seen many people come before him who were accused of fantastic crimes and had heard many bizarre allegations, the validity of which he now began to question. He was also a staunch Protestant, and, as such, took every opportunity to ridicule what he perceived to be the superstition and gullibility of the Catholic Church.

His most celebrated work, *A Discoverie of Witchcraft*, published in 1584, therefore, openly mocked the credulity of those who believed in witchcraft and attributed it to wretched and often mentally deficient people. He listed such beliefs as shape-changing and cursing, declaring that they had no basis in reality, and that those who believed in them often committed a greater crime than those whom they accused. Such "gross errors" were often the province of the Catholic Church, which only sought to foster such beliefs in order to maintain its power. He quoted Weyer and supported the German physician's assertion that those who were accused might have both social and mental problems in their everyday lives. His educated skepticism strengthened Weyer's suggestions and cast serious doubts on the common perceptions of both witchcraft and werewolfery as the 17th century dawned.

Full Moons

There was also another problem for such scientists and educated men to consider—the perceived connection between werewolves and the full moon. Although this is a slightly later idea than either Weyer or Scot, there is little doubt that werewolf transformations were viewed in the 17th and 18th centuries as being supernaturally influenced by the waxing and waning of the moon. In the 19th and 20th centuries this notion would be further developed, and the theme of a man being turned into a wolf would seemingly be dependent upon the lunar phases, although such an association never appeared in accounts of werewolf trials. Why did the notion of transformation then become associated with the full moon?

The moon, of course, has a long association with mental stability. Indeed, our own words *lunacy* and *lunatic* denoting mental illness or deterioration have their roots in *la lune*, the French word for the moon (originating from the name of the Roman goddess Luna). But where did such an association begin? The Greeks took a scientific notion of both the human body and illness, and, as the Roman Galen would do a little later, divided it up into various "humors" such as phlegm, blood, and bile, each specific to a certain bodily part. The exact balance of these allowed the body itself to function in a normal state and ensured good health. If these went out of kilter, then illness resulted—for instance, too much blood in the body would engender a fever. The brain, it was believed, contained large amounts of moisture, the balance of which was essential to its proper function. This allowed a civilized and rational train of thought to remain in ascendancy while other, dark impulses were kept restrained. However, as with other bodily parts, the internal workings of the body might also be influenced by some outside agency.

Noting the way in which the weak gravitational pull of the moon affected the tides of oceans, Greek physicians assumed that it had a similar affect upon the moisture that the brain contained, and it might throw the delicate "humoral balance" out of line and allow more savage and unwholesome lusts to come to the fore. The "civilized man" might be gradually transformed by the pull of the moon into a raging, irrational creature—a lunatic. Many Greek thinkers such as Aristotle and Hippocrates of Kos (460–370 BC) recounted it as a fact. Indeed, so strong was the association that the Greek goddess Selene (one representation of the triple moon-goddess) was identified with wild and unpredictable behavior and was sometimes depicted as dancing through the woodlands in an unrestrained and bizarre manner. Taking the writings of the Greeks as undeniable fact, Pliny the Elder (AD 23–78) brought such medical thinking to the Roman sphere.

Medicine

The world of medieval medicine was largely based on Greek and Roman thinking. It too based its remedies on the "humoral balances" of the body—for example, bleeding patients to reduce fevers and administering purges to rebalance phlegm and bile. It accepted unquestioningly the idea of the "moistness" of the brain and the effect that the moon might have upon it. Violent or feral behavior arose from an excess of fluid, which had accumulated within the skull and often resulted from the application of external forces such as the moon's "magnetic pull" upon the individual. Weak-willed, sinful, or physically deficient persons—those who were ill, malnourished, or who lived wretched lives—were especially susceptible to such behavior. This mode of thinking was also extended to include werewolf-type behavior—an individual vividly imagining that he or she was some sort of beast—as much as it did formal lunatics. This, argued the Church (which took an interest in everyday medicine because many of the early "doctors" were monks) was the indisputable result of sin—sinful people had deliberately exposed themselves to the baleful influences of the moon and had become feral and barbaric in their ways, believing themselves to be animals.

Gradually, Western medicine became influenced by thinking that emanated from the counties of the Middle East. As early as the 12th and 13th centuries, Crusaders returning from the Holy Land had brought back new perspectives and ideas particularly with regard to healing, which they had seen the Arabs practice there. Equally, texts by some of the Middle Eastern writers also began to circulate in the West, suggesting new ways of looking at illness. Arab writers such as Rashid-al-Din Hamdani (1247–1317) and Hakim Mohammed Amin of Lahijan (17th century), while holding firm to the teachings of the Koran, suggested that there might be more to mental illness than the dubious intervention of demons or the sins of the victim.

Even so, the idea of "humoral imbalance" and the effect of the moon upon the sufferer still persisted. In order to restore the body's natural rhythms, some doctors advised what became known as the "trepanning of the skull." This involved a small hole, known as a trepan or burr hole, in the skull (opinions as to where this should be drilled varied from physician to physician) in order to allow the excess moisture to drain out and restore the individual's senses. Ancient woodcuts and illustrations dating from the 16th century show a number of devices that might be used for this, some of which look more at home in a torture chamber. But even so there was much discussion about the effectiveness of the treatment, as some physicians, such as Moses Miamoides (1138–1204) and later Andreas Vesalius (1514–1564), argued that the only proper way to alleviate madness in an individual was to "bleed them" (that is, draw off a quantity of blood) to prevent "fevers and excitements" from inflaming the brain. This was especially efficacious; it was suggested, in the cases of some of those who believed themselves to be beasts and who craved human flesh, that an "excitement" was brought on by a surfeit of blood clouding the brain. The only way to relieve such cravings, it was said, was to "bleed" the patient or use leechcraft (the application of blood-sucking leeches).

Curiously, in old Sicilian folklore, the only way to "cure" a werewolf is to "bleed" it. In this tradition, werewolf blood is said to be black and has the consistency of tar; even taking the smallest amount from the veins of the beast would be enough to cleanse the victim from the curse. An old Sicilian folktale, supposedly based on a true incident at Palermo in 1889, illustrates this point.

Sicilian Folklore

A wealthy nobleman, living in either Palermo or Sapaparuta, was afflicted by the full moon. When it rose, he was supernaturally transformed into a ravening wolf and yielded to its lupine cravings for flesh. He trusted only one servant with his secret, and when he was so transformed, the man took him to the piazza and let him loose. There he would stalk those who were out at that time, killing several late-night revellers in the process. One night when he was wandering through the city, he encountered a soldier who was not afraid of him. He boldly faced the wolf, and, drawing his sword, slashed it across its face with the blade, cutting its forehead. Black, sticky blood spurted out.

It was only a small amount, for the sword blow had only been a glancing one, but it was enough to lift the werewolf curse. The creature fell, whining and crying at the soldier's feet, gradually changing back into its human form. The nobleman was incredibly happy and actually rewarded the soldier for releasing him from the terrible werewolf curse that had blighted him for so long.

Palermo

Two similar stories—one from Palermo and one from Ibla (Lower Ragusa), both involving the letting of blood to "cure" a werewolf, are also found in Sicilian folklore, showing the strength of the belief in that area.

The second tale involves a particularly religious woman from Palermo (some accounts give her as the sister of a priest—the sisters of the clergy were said to have special powers in many Catholic countries). Although she regularly attended Mass and fastidiously observed her prayers and devotions, these were not enough one night as she looked from the window of her house; she beheld a ferocious-looking wolf-like creature, crouching in the shadows nearby. It was certainly man-like, but it was covered in fur and had the snarling muzzle and gaping jaws of a wolf. Seeing her looking out, it emitted a roar and tried to climb up some growth on the house in order to get to her with its long and rending claws. In terror, the holy lady uttered prayers to St. Mary and St. Rosalie, but to no avail, for the werewolf had now reached her balcony and was climbing into the room. Fleeing back into the room, the woman grabbed a poniard (a lightweight dagger) and turned to face it. Issuing further prayers, she rammed the weapon at the advancing creature, catching it once again on the forehead. Thick, black, tarry blood welled up as, groaning and yelping in pain, the werewolf turned and fled. Here variants of the tale are told—some say that later, one of the woman's neighbors was found, half-naked nearby, whereas others say that the werewolf was actually a local prince who rewarded the woman with both money and jewels for releasing him from

the werewolf curse. No date is given for this encounter, but, similar to the earlier tale, it is said to have occurred during the latter half of the 19th century.

Ibla

The third, slightly older folktale from Ibla (lower Ragusa) concerns a priest who also confronted a werewolf. Ibla is a very old town that was heavily rebuilt as Ibla Ragusa following the great Sicilian earthquake of 1693. One of the oldest buildings that were rebuilt in the early 18th century is the church of Santa Maria della Scala (St. Mary of the Stairs), and it is this place of worship with which the holy man is associated. It appears that as he was crossing the piazza late at night, on his way back from some errand of mercy, he was confronted by the creature that had been lurking in the shadows. It bared its fangs and growled at him, and in the moonlight he was able to see that it was vaguely shaped like a man, but had all the attributes of a wolf, including a long and slavering muzzle. He offered up a prayer, but to no avail; in fact, the holy words seemed only to infuriate the beast that now threatened to maul him. He ran into the church, but the werewolf came after him, obviously not discomforted by the holy precincts. Close to the altar, the priest lifted a heavy cross and held it up. The werewolf did not appear fazed by the holy relic, but continued to advance threateningly, its jaws ominously drooling saliva. The priest retreated in front of it until his back was almost against the altar. In a wild attempt to save himself, the priest swung the cross before him like a weapon, striking the werewolf heavily on its forearm. Black, sticky blood oozed forth. The werewolf yelped like a dog and fled as its screams echoed all around the holy house. Before it reached the main door, it had begun to change. Eventually it collapsed on the steps of the church, and when the priest ran to offer help, he found himself staring into the face of a fellow cleric whom he knew.

Haltingly, the man told his story. He had been afflicted since childhood by the baleful rays of the moon, which transformed him into a savage beast; in that form he had prowled the old town, attacking and sometimes killing those whom he met. It was only the shedding of blood when struck by a blow from the heavy cross that had released him from the curse. In other versions of the same story it was a prominent benefactor to the Church who was revealed as the werewolf, although his name was never disclosed. Once again it was the rays of the full moon that caused the terrible transformation.

What is interesting about the latter two stories is that neither the prayers of the faithful nor the use of holy ornaments with all their significance seemed to affect the werewolf in question. Rather it is the violent drawing of blood that ultimately "cures" it. In cases the victims were the unwilling victims of the rays of the moon, helpless to avoid the transformation.

Moon Goddesses

There was, of course, another aspect to the moon's influence. It has already been noted that the full moon was believed to invoke the goddess Selene, who was its divine embodiment. However, Selene was only one aspect of the risen moon—indeed, she was only one part of a triple lunar goddess. Another incarnation of the same deity was the goddess Artemis (also known in the Roman world as Diana), who was associated throughout the ancient classical world, with the hunt. The majority of her hunting, given her connections with the moon (especially the full moon), was done at night, because this was also a time when a number of creatures hunted. Thus, those who were touched by the moon's rays (because Artemis was also connected to the moon) were seized with the hunting frenzy that characterized the goddess herself.

It was noted, even in ancient times, that the moon's rays seemed to have an excitable effect on dogs (which were a hunting animal), and this was sometimes put down to the goddess's influence. The goddess stirred the animals' hunting instincts and made them restless. The same might be done to certain types of individuals, especially the weak-willed and sinful. Thus, those who were wretched and steeped in sin might be subject to the moon's rays, as dogs were.

This baleful influence was linked to yet another aspect of the goddess, the incarnation known as Luna. This gave us our word *lunatic* to denote those whose behavior was either bizarre or unpredictable. Of course, no attempt was made to link such behavior to the distinct conditions under a full moon, except maybe for a change in the overall light. Although we are not absolutely certain, *this* may be partially responsible for changes in the behavior of certain animals. However, the wild and erratic behavior of the lunatics under the moon became associated with the savage characteristics of the werewolf, and it was assumed that the moon's rays might have an effect on a person and might actually trigger the transformation into the man-wolf. This rather dramatic idea would become more developed as writers and Hollywood movies turned their attention to the werewolf theme.

Elements of a Wolf

The links between lunacy, werewolfism, and wretched and sinful individuals grew as the Enlightenment progressed. During the late 17th and 18th centuries, men of learning began to question ideas that had formally been ignored by the Church—conditions such as demon possession, miracles, ghosts, vampires, and werewolves—seeking some sort of scientific or rational answer. Rather than attributing werewolfism to a possession of the individual and possession by malign supernatural forces thinkers, followers of Weyer began to associate it with madness, or at least with some form of mental abnormality. They discounted items such as magic belts, wolfskin robes, or even diabolic unguents and potions, and began to look for more natural reasons why this condition should have been brought about. What causes, they asked, might make an individual believe he or she was a ravening animal?

Plants

Some suggested that the reason might be that individuals had somehow ingested elements that had affected their brains. Such elements might have included mushrooms or fungi, which formed a part of the diet of some country folk. Or it might be simply inhaling the perfume of some woodland plant that might then produce hallucinations. One of those plants that was strongly associated with wolves and the like was aconite (aconitum), which grew in profusion in many European woodland areas. This plant was known by many names—Devil's helmet, monkshood, woman's bane, devils bile—and had been associated with witchcraft. Initially it was thought that this growth might be responsible for the hallucination of changing into a wolf, as it was considered to be one of the central ingredients of magical unguents or salves, which were supposedly used for that purpose. It was also used in the preparation of poisons (aconitine), which was closely associated with sorcerous practices (at one time the acts of poisoning and witchcraft were almost synonymous), and therefore with sin, wickedness, and aberrant behavior. The poison is now known to affect the nervous system and can produce sweats, cramps, tremors, nervous pain, and perhaps even hallucinations, which might include the belief that someone was transforming into an animal. The plant was said to be most effective when it was a flower, and it was then that the most wolf transformations occurred. Later, however, it was considered that the reverse might be true, because the plant was actually said to repel wolves—giving it the name by which it is more commonly known: wolfsbane.

Those who were most susceptible to the effects of such plants, it was also believed, were the poor who often lived in the wilds, beyond the pale of civilization. They often subsisted on plants and fungi, and it was only natural that their sinful condition interacted with some of the plants they ate to turn them into wolves (or, perhaps more properly, to imagine that they were wolves).

Psychology

Despite 17th- and 18th-century speculation concerning herbs and fungi, the main contention remained that these unfortunates were simply deluded. Although this idea formed the first stirrings of a perspective on mental health, such concepts were still slightly beyond most thinkers. The delusion was not wholly ascribed to mental defects, but to the intervention of the Evil One in wretched and unwholesome lives. If people believed they were and acted like wolves, it was because the Devil excited the animal passions within their bodies in order to deny them access to Heaven. The psychiatric notion of "hysteria" was unknown in these early times, and would not come to fruition for almost 200 years in the writings of a later figure, Sigmund Freud, who was widely regarded as the father of psychoanalysis. In 1897, Freud, who had turned his attention to a number of alleged werewolf cases, developed a theory that the "hysteria," which was now beginning to be suggested as an explanation for such cases, might be a delayed emotional reaction to an earlier sexual abuse or to infantile sexual fantasies, which had been repressed. He paid particular attention to the Grenier case of 1603, which seemed to bear out some of these theories, as did some aspects of the Gandillion trial.

Freud may, of course, have been influenced by some of Weyer's work, and there is no doubt that he had read his texts—he cited the German's writings among his 10 most influential books during an interview in 1906. And, according to his own account, he found himself face to face with a patient who exhibited some of the same characteristics that were prevalent during the French werewolf trials.

Indeed, for the purposes of keeping his actual identity secret, Freud named him as the Wolf Man in both his notes and accounts of the meeting. However, the patient is described as a rather well-to-do man from a wealthy Russian family who, during the course of his analysis, described a persistent dream that he'd had in infancy concerning wolves. In the dream, he was lying in bed in his own bedroom when suddenly a nearby window had opened, and, getting up, he looked out to see several wolves—about six or seven of them—lying at the foot of a large walnut tree outside, looking back at him extremely intently. None of the creatures made a move nor threatened him, but all the same, their very presence terrified the boy, who screamed, woke himself up, and had to be comforted by his nurse. There was also a folk element to the story of which both Freud and his patient were well aware. There was, in both Romanian and Russian lore, a tradition concerning an individual known as the Wolf Master, sometimes depicted as a kind of hybrid creature who dwelt in the forest and who had control over the wolf packs there. This being was not all human, and often experienced the same lusts and appetites as the wolves themselves. In his book *Were-wolf and Vampire in Romania* (1982), Professor Harry Senn describes such a creature as actually hunting with the carious wolf packs through the forest and being treated more or less as their leader. The Wolf Master was normally shown as sitting in some woodland glade surrounded by wolves at rest, and perhaps Freud's patient considered

himself in this guise rather than as an actual ravening werewolf. There was also another element; the patient had been born on December 25 (Christmas Day). There was also an ancient Christian tradition that said those who dared to be born on the birthday of Christ were destined to become monsters and agents of the Devil. The patient had also been born with a caul (a translucent membrane across the face, which can usually be removed immediately after birth), but, nevertheless was an ill omen in many parts of Russia. (Conversely, it is considered to be a sign of good luck and a sign that the person will never die by drowning or by fire in many other cultures).

Freud also notes that the nurse who attended the boy in his infant years was extremely religious and deeply superstitious, and took the caul as a signal that the child would grow up to become a werewolf and an agent of the Devil. She continually imparted this feeling on her infant, together with a number of old legends concerning the Wolf Master out in the forests. Thus, in the patient's mind, the figures of the wolves took on an added and sinister significance. Freud's analysis suggested that the child was probably suffering from an innate desire to return to the womb—completely dismissing the supernatural and folk elements that had been passed on by the nurse (although he did acknowledge the part they had played in the formulation of the subconscious imagery of the dream). There is an interesting footnote to this: Freud was born with a caul.

Behavior

Freud was, of course, not the only thinker to attribute the alleged werewolf experience, and some individuals claimed he had the mental "hysteria." The French doctor Jean Martin Charcot (1825–1893), sometimes described as the "father of neurology," recognized the connection. Although he did not refer specifically to the French werewolf cases, he suggested that the condition might be ascribed to the "excitement" of hereditary nervous conditions. As a physician (and later professor of neuropathology) at the Saltpetriere Hospital—a Paris hospital for poor women, Charcot dealt with many violent "hysterics," some of whom displayed elements of animalistic behavior. Some of the descriptions of the patients whom he treated might well correspond to what might be loosely termed as "werewolf behavior," and these Charot tried to help through a relatively new medical procedure: hypnotherapy. Indeed, he is now seen as one of the first medical men to use hypnosis in the treatment of the mentally disturbed.

Sufferers

The enquiry into the "werewolf behavior" by eminent and learned medical men marked a subtle shift in how the condition was perceived. Formerly, it had often been viewed as a deliberate, malignant event, perpetrated by sorcerers and witches in order to satisfy their own evil ends, using magical equipment or potions, such as belts, wolfskin cloaks, or specific unguents. The writers of the *Malleus* had railed against witches in the employ of the Devil, who attacked their neighbors in the guise of wolves and other animals. The Age of Reason changed that and moved the idea away from the idea of a premeditated act of sorcery, witchcraft, or Black Magic, which had been previously held by the Church. No longer was werewolfery invariably seen as a part of witchcraft, and rather than a deliberate act of defiance against God, it was perceived as an almost involuntary affliction, which had been brought about in an almost accidental fashion. The werewolf was depicted almost as a "sufferer" who often fought against his or her transformation, which often occurred in response to the rising of the moon or the inhaling of a plant such as wolfsbane. As in the case of the vampire, the bite of a werewolf was enough to turn its victim into a ravening animal when the moon was at its height. This notion of an involuntary and often dramatic transformation would later be picked up by Hollywood as the basis of a number of its films, which in turn strengthened and fixed the perception in the public mind. In most of these, the protagonist was usually an unfortunate who had been stricken with the "werewolf curse"—synonymous with the idea of disease—in some way or another, and was "forced" to become a wolf or wolf-like humanoid in some dramatic and spectacular transformation. A stark distinction was usually drawn for the purposes of dramatic effect between the civilized, gentle man and the ravening, voracious animal; the main theme of a number of the early films often concentrated on efforts to delay the transformation or to rid the individual of the "curse" or "sickness." As the 18th century drew to a close, the idea of the werewolf had been more or less transformed from the practitioner of evil to that of an unfortunate victim. As society gradually sought to understand the outsider, or those who were different or strange the idea of the werewolf became bathed in a rather more sympathetic light.

Feral Creatures

Before considering the ideas put forward by the cinematic representations of the creature, however, it is necessary to consider another grouping that some societies considered to be as different as the "lunatics." These were the feral individuals—those who had been raised in the wild, often by specific animals or animal groupings—who surfaced into the civilized social mainstream from time to time.

Leaders

It has already been noted earlier that in popular tradition, the brothers Romulus and Remus (the twin founders of Rome) were suckled and raised by a she-wolf. This could be counted as an early acknowledgement of feral children returning to society. However, the Roman founders were not the only children of ancient legend to have been reared by wolves. A Turkish tale of great antiquity tells how the Turkish nation came to be. It tells how the ancestors of the Turks were all killed in a massive battle, all except for one small boy who was hidden in a marsh for safety. With his kinsmen dead, the child was now left alone, but was found by a she-wolf who took him back to her lair and raised him with her cubs. He grew to adulthood and had intercourse with her, and, as a result she gave birth to 10 sons, one of whom was Assena, the great leader among the Turks of Turkistan, who used a wolf's head as his emblem.

In Persia, the great warrior leader Zal was carried off as an infant by a giant bird, which took the child as prey, but ended up nurturing it. In seventh-century China, the wise and cunning Tseu Ouen (the governor of Tch'ou Province) was allegedly abandoned by his mother—a daughter of the Prince of Iun—but was subsequently raised by a tigress brought back to the Imperial Court by the prince. The child was given the nickname *Teou jeou ou t'ou*, which means "Teou who was raised by the tiger." It was later shortened into his formal name. He was regarded as very wise and politically astute, but was also subject to fierce tempers—all of which was attributed to his rearing in the wild and to his tigress protector.

And there are other stories too (whether true or myth) from a number of other ancient cultures concerning kings and mighty warriors who had been raised by animals in the wild and who had ultimately returned to lead their people or to found powerful civilizations. There are also a number of legends concerning such leaders indulging in great cannibalistic feasts, which had more in common with their wild origins than civilized society. Assena, for example, is supposed to have been prepared to eat his enemies whom he had defeated in battle. In the cases of such ancient heroes who had been raised in the wild, prowess in battle was usually matched with intense savagery.

Saints

The imagery of the feral child continued even into the Christian tradition with several notable saints being associated with the idea. St. Albeus (Ailbhe) was allegedly abandoned as a baby in the wilds by his mother who had given birth to him "unlawfully" (possibly through incest). A she-wolf, foraging for food, discovered the infant and reared him as her own until he was discovered by a shepherd named Lochanus, who sold him to some Britons. He would later accept Christianity, founding a number of churches and monasteries (including one in the Arran Islands where St. Enda was abbot) and eventually traveled to Rome.

A great number of miracles are attributed to him (including several concerning animals), and he is supposedly the saint who baptised St. David of Wales. During medieval times he was widely regarded as the patron saint of Munster. It is also said that at one point the she-wolf who had suckled him came to seek his protection from some nobles who were hunting her. The saint granted her protection and turned the pursuing nobles away, and for the rest of her life the wolf came to his hermitage, often bringing her cubs, every day. Indeed, in some representations of the saint, both as an important Bishop and patron of Munster, he is depicted with a she-wolf lying at his feet, denoting, perhaps, his feral origins.

The province of Munster was, of course, famous for its wolves, and during medieval times was the location of the famous black and tan wolf hunt, which progressed all through the province and drew many of the early Irish aristocracy. The depiction of its patron saint in the company of the animals may well be used to reflect this.

Also in Irish Christian mythology the father of the Irish St. Barre was supposedly reared by wolves following his abandonment by his mother after an incestuous birth. In Bordeaux, France, the fifth-century St. Medoc was reputedly raised by a hunting she-wolf who had carried him away from his cradle and into the wild. Perhaps she had intended to devour him, but actually ended up nurturing him as her own. However, it is said that even in mature years and long after his return to civilization, the saint displayed a number of lupine characteristics, which hinted at his life in the wild.

Wild Boy of Aveyron

In more recent times, one of the most famous and perhaps best documented of all feral children, the celebrated "Wild Boy of Aveyron," made his appearance in France, during the Enlightenment. In 1797, a young boy was seen running naked through the woods in the mountainous Lacaune region of the country. The following year, he was captured and taken to be an exhibit named "the wild boy from Aveyon" after the governmental department in which he'd been captured. However, he eventually escaped and returned to the wild, and for 15 months a number of people tried to track him down and recapture him. He was frequently seen, living wild in the forests, and was said to have constructed several lairs, which were later found abandoned. For some time he managed to stay ahead of his pursuers, but in 1799 he was again captured by hunters in the woods of St. Semin sur Rance, who sympathetically gave him into the care of an old widow. He could not speak, but made low grunting noises, so it was impossible to determine his origins. He would not eat meat, and preferred raw acorns, chestnuts, walnuts, berries, and potatoes.

Shortly after he was placed with the widow, he escaped again into the nearby mountains. However, the exposed slopes were rather different from the relative comfort of the forest, and they offered little shelter. A particularly severe winter closed in and the boy was forced to travel between the isolated mountain farms hunting for food and warmth. He traveled across the broad plateau that lies between Lacaune and Roqueceziere where many kind farmers

gave him raw potatoes and shelter—offers that he always seemed to refuse. In January 1800, he was hunted down and captured again, and this time he was taken to a local orphanage. Examined by the authorities, he was surmised to be somewhere between 12 and 15 years of age, although little else could be determined. He refused to wear clothes, and shortly after admission, he began to utter small human-like cries, even though he had remained steadfastly silent when brought to the orphanage. For a short time he refused to eat, and when food was placed in front him, he smelled it suspiciously like an animal before taking only the smallest morsel. Hearing of his capture and confinement, many people came to see him, but it became apparent that large crowds frightened him, and he often tried to bite anybody who ventured too close to him.

This was, of course, the Age of Reason when all sorts of explanations were being sought for what had been previously considered inexplicable, and naturally the captivity of the "Wild Boy" created much interest in learned circles. There had been some writings on feral children before—in the works of Theodore Rousseau and Pierre Etienne de Condillac for example—but the Wild Boy offered a study of such an individual in regulated and confined circumstances.

One of those who took a specific interest in the case of the Wild Boy was a young physician named Jean Itard, who worked closely with the Abbe Sicard, director of the National Institute for Deaf Mutes, and who was a student of the early psychiatrist Philippe Pinel. Pinel was not particularly interested in the Wild Boy, and as chairman of a distinguished committee who examined the boy, he declared him to be a "congenital idiot," casting doubts on his feral origins. It was also assumed that the child was profoundly deaf; Itard disagreed. Sicard's institute had done some work in the treatment and education of deaf mutes in the years following the French Revolution, and Itard was certain that the boy was not simply retarded or insane as the committee had claimed. He volunteered to look after the boy (whom he now named Victor) and to embark on a regime of education that had been developed at the institute. It soon became apparent that Victor was not deaf at all, but that he had been injured at some stage (either accidentally or deliberately), as there was a huge horizontal mark across his throat. Itard assumed that this had been inflicted by whomever had originally abandoned the child in the forest to prevent him from crying and drawing attention. However, if this were true, the cut had been made clumsily and had not damaged the larynx, which meant that theoretically Victor was able to speak. Excitedly Itard attempted to teach Victor to speak and continued to do so throughout a number of years. Initially he appeared to be successful, but gradually Victor seemed to lose interest and progress became difficult.

The boy lived at home with Itard and his housekeeper Madam Guerin, and though he displayed some signs of civilization, he would from time to time revert to more animalistic behavior. For example, he still ate using his hands and from time to time fought with the family dogs over a bone. However, when he found Madam Guerin weeping following the death of her husband, Victor clearly showed both sympathy and emotion. Itard thought this was a major breakthrough, stating that it showed that Victor was essentially human, and redoubled his efforts to develop and educate the boy, although, it has to be said, without much success. Victor, the Wild Boy of Aveyron died in Paris in 1828, bringing his case to a close. Despite Itard's best efforts, he had never really learned to speak, and his origins still remain more or less unknown.

If he had done nothing else, Victor provoked and stimulated interest and debate about feral individuals and what actually separated men from wild animals. His case has provided the basis for numerous books, films (such as Francois Truffaut's classic *L'Enfant Sauvage* in 1970), and studies, including one by American Dr. Harlan Lane of Boston University, a psychotherapist working with language, speech, and education. In 1977 Lane stated that although Victor remained unable to speak until his death, certain flaws in Itard's technique (some of which were later corrected with other deaf and mute patients) were probably responsible for the Wild Boy's lack of communication. German neurologist Uta Frith has even suggested that Victor may well have been suffering from a form of autism.

For many thinkers and physicians, including Pinel, it was the gift of rational speech that distinguished men from the beasts, because speech demonstrated logical and rational cognitive processes. Therefore, even though Victor *looked* like a man, he was retarded, and closer to the beasts, because he was not capable of such speech. The fact that Victor growled and snarled, coupled with his almost bestial behavior, amply demonstrated this in many peoples' eyes. In the case of the Wild Boy, the line between man and animal, and between lunatic and animal, was very blurred.

Other Sightings

Although Victor, the Wild Boy, is probably the best documented case of a feral upbringing, there were many others. The French philosopher Jean-Jacques Rousseau sited a number of examples of children raised by wild creatures, such as a wolf-child raised in Hesse, Germany, in 1344, and the bear-child of Lithuania in 1694. In addition, there was the famous case of Peter of Hanover, a feral child estimated at around 15 years of age, who had been captured in

1724 in the Hertswold Forest near the German town of Hamlin (of Pied Piper fame). Similar to Victor, he could not speak and was living among the forest trees "like a squirrel," subsisting on berries and nuts. The wild boy excited great interest at the time and drew the attention of the English King George I during one of his visits to Hanover. Peter was brought to London where he became the subject of much curiosity and of a biting satire by the writer Jonathan Swift. He died in 1785, and lived to a relatively great age, and he was buried in the churchyard at St. Mary's, Northchurch in Hertfordshire. Even though he and Victor were among the most famous of the feral children, others continued to surface from time to time. The most controversial was the case of Kamala and Amala, the Wolf Girls of Godamuri in India during the early years of the 20th century.

Kamala and Amala

In 1926, a local clergyman and head of an Indian orphanage, the Reverend Joseph Amrita Lal Singh, wrote to the *Calcutta Statesman,* recounting the extraordinary tale of two small Indian girls that had been in his care. The Reverend Singh claimed that he had been approached by a man from Godamuri, a village in the province of Midnapore, who said that he had something interesting to show him. Upon visiting the man's house, the Reverend Singh was taken to a cage set up close by in which there were two small, savage-looking girls; the man claimed he had captured them in the forests nearby. Later, Singh would claim that he'd captured them himself in October 1920 when he took them from a wolf pit where they'd appeared to have been raised by the animals. He took them back to the orphanage where he attempted to raise them. In all the time that they were there, he kept a "diary" (little more than a series of loose pages), which recorded his efforts to "humanize" the children. In this, he claimed that the girls exhibited wolf-like behavior—they refused to wear clothes, they scratched and bit anyone who ventured close to them, they would not eat cooked food, but devoured raw meat with gusto, and they went about on all fours like animals. Indeed, they had calluses on both feet and hands from this activity, so they must have traveled in this fashion for a considerable time. The Reverend Singh named the eldest Kamala, who looked to be about eight years old. The youngest was Amala, who was thought to be about 18 months to two years old. Neither of the girls spoke, so they were not able to indicate where they came from or how they came to be living with wolves.

According to the Reverend Singh, both children displayed odd sleep patterns, waking around midnight to prowl about, occasionally howling with what Singh described as a "wolf-like cry." Physically they displayed the darkened skin and broad faces and noses of aboriginal peoples of that region of India, but their bodies appeared to be stunted, and they went about with a kind of bowed, loping motion. They had no idea of personal hygiene, and they relieved themselves publicly whenever they felt the urge, often dragging their bottoms along the ground as dogs sometime will after defecation. Singh thought this was an attempt to rid themselves of worms, in the style of canines, rather than as an attempt to clean themselves.

They appeared to show little interest in human company, but took more to the animals around the orphanage, especially the dogs. They seemed to enjoy their meat raw, shunning anything cooked, as well as berries and fruit, and drank milk from a bowl placed on the ground, like a dog. According to Singh, they also ingested grass, small pebbles, and bits of dirt in the way that some dogs might. However, when given raw meat still on the bone, they proceeded to clean the bone with their hands and did not gnaw it off as carnivorous animals would.

In 1921, Amala became ill and died from a possible kidney infection. Kamala, according to the Reverend Singh's notes, showed visible signs of mourning and thereafter became much more approachable, building a relationship with some of the other orphanage children, a cat, and a hyena cub that was being raised on the premises. She became more used to the company of adult human beings, became better house trained, and was able to walk upright for short distances, although she frequently resorted to walking around on all fours. From time to time Singh claimed that she would revert to wolf-like behavior. For example, when a cow died near the orphanage and was surrounded by vultures, the girl chased the birds away and began to eat the raw flesh of the carcass with her hands, chewing on the bones as well. She died in 1929 of what appears to have been uraemia (renal failure).

The case of the wild girls caused a great deal of controversy, mainly due to the fact that most of the evidence for their condition and behavior lay in the Reverend Singh's notes, which were often contradictory. Much of the "evidence" for their "wolfism" came from his own uncorroborated observations, and this led some doctors and psychiatrists to speculate that many of them were fabricated. Many of the accounts (given solely by Singh) were so conflicting and at variance with medical knowledge that most scientists believed that the girls had not been raised by wolves at all, and that this was a ploy by the Reverend Singh to promote his orphanage. Indeed, it was suggested that they may have suffered from congenital disorders and had been abandoned by their parents—a practice not uncommon in that part of India. There were also scientific inaccuracies in some of the accounts, and no one was able to verify the wolf pit where Singh claimed he had found the children. Subsequent advances in behavioral science have led a number of modern-day authorities to suggest that the girls were not "wolf children" at all, but rather unfortunates suffering from some sort of congenital affliction coupled with behavioral problems. Although not denying that the children actually existed, the idea of them being raised by wolves has been more or less dismissed. However, from time to time, even into the modern era, feral individuals—mainly young people—continue to emerge.

Wolf Connections

Although it is not proposed to give a detailed examination of connections and problems between feral children, the notion of such "foundlings" had a profound influence on the perception of the werewolf. This came about in two ways: First, it blurred the distinction between man and animal to an even greater degree. Did the primal beast continue to lurk, somewhere beneath the sophisticated veneer of even the most civilized man, and might it be called forth by environment or circumstance? In the 19th century, society struggled with this concept. The works of Charles Darwin (1809–1882) were now challenging—and continue to do so—the central tenets of the Church teaching by asserting that man, formerly believed to have been specifically created by God, was in fact not all that far removed from chimpanzees. (Even during the late 17th and 18th centuries, explorers in places such as Borneo had described hairy and monkey-like "men" living in the forests—they may have been describing orangutans.) Was it possible that man could "revert" to his animalistic origins under certain circumstances?

The second way in which the feral children influenced the "werewolf perception" was that it reinforced the idea that the condition was a "curse" or a "misfortune." It is quite probable that many of these "feral foundlings" were either congenitally afflicted or perhaps "retarded" in some way, and this had led to their abandonment in the wild by their parents. Their behavior in human company resulted from these deficiencies and by the wildness of their accidental upbringing. They were not to be held responsible for it—they in fact were the "victims" of the situation. This in some ways strengthened the connections between feral behavior and "lunacy"—a connection that had already been established, and had a "knock-on" effect concerning the perception of werewolves. Rather than becoming werewolves or feral creatures for evil purposes or at the behest of the Devil, the individual became a victim of the werewolf curse against his or her will. Indeed, the werewolf strain was tenuously becoming associated with madness. The rays of the full moon, it was said, affected lunatics, but it also turned afflicted individuals into ravening beasts, so they were not really responsible for their actions. Their change from man to beast was often both involuntary and dramatic.

Werewolves in Film

The idea of the "victim" with his or her dramatic transformation (usually under the moon's baleful influence) was, of course, ripe for commercial exploitation, and was quickly taken up by Hollywood. In the 1930s cinema was rapidly becoming one of the most popular forms of entertainment, and one of its most popular genres was horror. The classic movie *Dracula*, starring the sinister Bela Lugosi, together with *Frankenstein* starring the Englishman William Henry Pratt were among the leading money-making films of their day. In order to extend the genre (and make more money), the film companies searched around for a new horror character, and they found it in the werewolf.

In the 1930s through to the early 1940s, one of the leading companies in the movie world was Universal Studios, who had released both *Dracula* and *Frankenstein* to critical acclaim in 1931. Determined to repeat the success of these "monster movies," they released *Werewolf of London* in 1935, but it enjoyed only a modest success. Universal decided that it needed a real blockbuster if they were to repeat earlier successes. With little expense spared they released *The Wolf Man* in 1941, which brought the image of the werewolf to cinema audiences everywhere. There were problems, however. The film company had planned to use either Lugosi or Karloff (who had now become household names in the world of horror and beyond) in the central role, but both were committed elsewhere. The man Universal finally chose was cast in a slightly different vein—not a huge, hulking figure or a sinister, brooding presence—and he was an actor of more moderate talent. His name was Creighton Chaney and he was the son of legendary silent movie actor Lon Chaney. Perhaps recognizing his son's acting limitations, Lon had advised him not to take up film work. However, Creighton was determined to make his career in the cinema and, not one to discard a family connection, changed his name to Lon Chaney, Jr., after his father's death in 1931. Even though his was not an accomplished horror actor in the style of Lugosi or Karloff, he had rugged, brutish looks, which was coupled with an almost child-like innocence; such a combination suited the tone of the film and made him a hit. He was ideal as the figure of the cursed man who was the film's central character.

However, *The Wolf Man* suffered a distinct disadvantage. The company's other two successes, *Dracula* and *Frankenstein*, had been based on classic books by Bram Stoker and Mary Shelley, with which at least part of the audience were familiar. Those who were not familiar could go and buy the novels and relive the excitement in their own homes. There was no real equivalent literary work associated with the werewolf, and so the film had to stand on its own plot and on Chaney's performance. The scriptwriter was Clifford Siodmak who came from an established horror screenwriting family. In order to strengthen the plot, Universal introduced some folkloric elements—both real and contrived—into the story. Although many of the alleged instances of werewolf activity occurred in France, in order to link the movie to Universal's other successes, the creature becomes largely confined to Germany and parts of Eastern Europe. It postulated the idea that a man might become a werewolf under the rays of the full moon, but only if he'd been bitten by another such creature. This, of course, had no basis in folklore, but fit in well with the idea of vampirism as promoted in the film *Dracula*.

Werewolves

Siodmak also introduced the idea that a werewolf could only be killed by a silver bullet—an idea that supposedly belonged to Romanian gypsy lore; it was nothing of the sort. Although werewolves did exist in Romanian and Russian gypsy tradition, they were not a significant terror. Indeed, ordinary wolves were usually regarded with much more apprehension, because it was believed that the werewolf still had the *soul* of a human being, which was good. French tradition, as had already been noted, was much more antipathetic toward the idea of the werewolf than gypsy society, but of course that did not fit well with the Universal cinematic catalogue. Siodmak also suggested that the werewolf could be repelled (as was the vampire) by showing it a crucifix or by drawing (or carrying) a protective pentagram such as a Romany talisman. Again, there is no real basis for this in Romany tradition, but it certainly added to the dramatic atmosphere of the film, giving a sort of mystical edge to the storyline.

The Wolf Man established two main elements that would become part of later werewolf tradition. First, it solidified the idea that the werewolf was often a victim of some fatal curse, which was activated as soon as the full moon (or the new moon) rose. Chaney's almost child-like innocence established him firmly as one living in terror of a terrible transformation, but who could do very little about it. Second, the "victim" would not fully become a wolf in the transformation, but rather morph into some form of hybrid creature that was part man and part wolf. The nature of this being was, however, incredibly ferocious and feral, and owed nothing to its human origins, wholly reflecting the animalistic element. In later films, the protagonist would often have no recollection of the events that occurred after transformation.

There were, of course, a number of problems with this approach—the resolution of some of these was shown with dramatic effect by subsequent films. For example, what was the actual transformation (was it "possession"

by a wolf spirit in the style of Voodoo or of Native American beliefs?); what happened if the rays of the moon did not touch the individual (would that prevent the transformation, or would he or she change anyway as soon as the moon had risen?); could the transformation actually be stopped by a cleric? All these questions would form the basis of the movies that were to follow in the wake of *The Wolf Man*.

Although vampire movies continued to dominate the horror genre, there were also a good number of werewolf films as well. Throughout the 1940s and early 1950s they continued to appear sporadically, and by the 1960s, with the emergence of Christopher Lee as Dracula, they were becoming something of a rarity. One or two achieved something of a cult status. In 1957, American International Pictures released *I Was a Teenage Werewolf* directed by Herman Cohen and starring Michael Landon as a troubled teenager struggling to come to terms with his lycanthropy. The film was a success among the youth audience, but not so much among the older movie-goers, as Landon's brooding teenage menace was quite disturbing at the time and suggested animalistic overtones lurking among the rebellious young. Nevertheless, werewolf films continued to be made, keeping the werewolf in the public mind. Arguably one of the most celebrated was John Landis's 1981 *An American Werewolf in London*, which a number of critics hailed as "a masterpiece." Well written and directed, the story incorporates many of the elements that have come from the 1930s in an absorbing, fresh, and exciting way, which unquestioningly made the film a box-office success. It was followed in 1994 by *Wolf* starring Jack Nicholson, which showed that werewolf films could draw big stars. It too did well at the box office.

Another area in which the werewolf genre developed was the pornographic film industry. The sexual element contained in both *American Werewolf* and *Wolf* had perhaps proved popular among the cinema-going public, and pornographic filmmakers took this up. There was another slant too. In 1945, during the final days of World War II, Adolph Hitler had ordered the formation of what became known as the Werwolf (Wehrwulf) Brigade—a group of German partisans who unsuccessfully tried to halt the Russian advance into Germany. Certain film directors took up the theme of girls in Nazi uniform and equated them with werewolves. Thus, films with such titles as *Nazi Wolf Girls* and *Sex Wolves of the Third Reich* began to appear in the pornography market, many made by American and Italian directors.

Whether they involved large-breasted women in Nazi uniforms or not, the films kept the werewolf in popular culture. Films such as *American Werewolf*, of course, prompted imitations in other fields, and comics such as *Werewolf By Night* (produced by Marvel Comics) enjoyed something of a success in the mid-to-late 1980s. Vampires, however, continued to dominate, with the likes of *Buffy the Vampire Slayer* (both a film and TV series) and the more recent *Twilight* series. To some extent, the werewolf was more or less pushed into the background as far as public appetite was concerned. The bloody frenzy that characterized many werewolf films now began to appear in the so-called "slasher movies" where the violence and gore were conducted by deranged humans rather than hybrid wolf-like monsters. Nonetheless, the lurking presence in the forests still continues to haunt the human mind, and the thin, high-pitched cry of a wolf echoing from among the distant hills can still make the blood run cold. The shadow of the wolf still hasn't gone away.

Conclusion: Fangs Ain't What They Used to Be

Even a man who's pure in heart,
And who says his prayers at night,
Can become a wolf when the wolfsbane blooms,
And the Autumn moon is bright.

—*The Wolf Man*, 1935

From the ancient cave paintings of the Pyrenees to the modern-day American silver screen, the idea of the werewolf seems to have come a long way. To some extent, the being has been somewhat pushed to the periphery in much of the horror genre, with prominence being given to vampires or CGI mummies. Somewhere deep in the recesses of folklore, however, the creature still lurks, and is still available to those who wish to hunt for it. Its origins lie in the beliefs and imaginings of prehistoric hunters, who viewed the ferocity and hunting prowess of the wolf with a mixture of terror and envy. They thought that by mimicking the traits of the animal and by donning skins and other accoutrements relating to it, they could acquire similar skills and ferocity for themselves. Perhaps they even believed that a wolf-spirit would descend on them and possess them, making them as ferocious as the creature itself—that was not an illogical step to take. And so the idea of being possessed by the werewolf and the transformation of man into beast was formulated.

The werewolf or beast-man embodied a mixture of emotions and perceptions in early societies—the everyday man who was a member of his community would become the feared and ferocious hunter under the influence of the wild beast. He was worthy of admiration, even awe, but also fear, as in his ferocious, unreasoning beast-like state, he might also turn against his neighbors. And in a time when mankind was beginning to differentiate itself from the animal kingdom out of which it had emerged, the beast-man provided a stark and savage reminder of an animalistic past. For many emergent civilizations this was probably a rather uncomfortable memory, and as mankind became more settled, stories of savage half-bestial creatures, perhaps living in far-off lands, gnawed at the very edges of sophisticated society and created nightmares for more modern men.

And yet there was probably another element to the figure of the beast-man, for, conversely, it also represented freedom—the thrill of the hunt together with the absence of the constraints of a more regimented culture. It was wildness; it was the exhilaration that civilized men imagined existed within the bestial world. It accorded hidden passions and concealed rages, as it shook off the very trappings of what made mankind "civilized." Such a deep-seated

longing was often shown in the images and reliefs of classical hunting god-desses who were usually accompanied by wolves or wolf-like beings as a reminder of the chase. There was also an element of power in the ideal, for these bestial rages often gave warriors success in battle and caused terror among the ranks of their enemies—consequently, many great heroes of former times were accorded "wolf-like" outbursts, and these became a part of their legend. Indeed, as we have seen, there were whole companies of ancient warriors who experienced such wild behavior—the berserkers (those who wore the "bear shirts" and were transformed by them) of Nordic tradition, for instance. And the beast-man motif, particularly that of a man changing into a wolf, became the central focus of many medieval lays and ballads, with the transformed man often as the hero of such tales. And yet the notion of wild-ness and unpredictability—of unfettered and uncontrolled fierceness—still lay at the center of the idea, placing the wereman well beyond the pale of good-ness and order.

Small wonder, then, that structured organizations such as the Church viewed the concept of the beast-man with a mixture of horror and dismay. For the clerics, the creature represented all that was feral and dark in the human soul and served as a forceful reminder of the Pagan past. The beast-man was an agent of the Devil, and such creatures in faraway lands had been placed there by the Evil One to lure God's children from the path of righteousness. Even so, as the clergy went on, there were those living closer to home that would perform the same function and might actually turn on the Godly and kill them. These were witches and sorcerers who dwelt among the community, but who were covertly beasts striving to do harm to their neighbors at the behest of the Devil himself. They allowed their bestial side to come out, argued the Church, either through the use of some magical artifact (given to them by the Devil or

Conclusion

his minions) or by the use of charms, spells, potions, or unguents that they used in secret against those around them.

Such teachings had a profound effect on early society, for it meant that those who were isolated, old, or different from mainstream society, or who might have had peculiar ways about them, or who were just widely disliked, were immediately suspect. The belief also moved the idea of the beast-man away from the heroic hunter/warrior figure to the skulking creature that lurked in the forests and that attacked the righteous at will and with incalculable ferocity. It was a creature of sin and darkness, or at least, so the Christian clergy said.

These two elements—the lonely and eccentric individuals living on or beyond the periphery of normal society, and the demonic, shaggy wolf-like being—readily merged in the public imagination, particularly through certain werewolf trials, especially in France. As with witches, those who were "different" or followed unusual lifestyles were imagined by their neighbors (and by the civil authorities) to be werewolves and could take the form of the wolf for demonic purposes when they chose. This was also linked with notions of cannibalism (which probably did occur in some remote regions) and sexual depravity, which was perhaps used to characterize "outsiders" by a community.

The harshness of the werewolf trials in France, which came on the edge of the Enlightenment, together with the seeming wretchedness of the lives of many of the accused, provoked deep debate and consideration among medical men and those of learning. They even engendered serious study and some sympathy, leading to the idea that those who became werewolves might not necessarily be agents of the Devil at all, but rather the victims of some curse, either supernatural or medical. And this idea would gradually become the paramount one as the Enlightenment progressed and would continue into modern

times. Rather than being viewed as a malefic sorcerer, the werewolf was now seen as a victim of some dreaded condition. There was also a perceived attachment to mental instability. This linked it inevitably to the moon, the rays of which were believed to excite both the mentally weak and the insane, giving rise to the term *lunatic*. Some of the more dramatic transformations into beasts were said to occur under those same baleful rays. The drama of such transformation was, of course, played up by those who wrote about them in books and by later American filmmakers. Many of the books and films dealt with the efforts of the perceived victim to delay or even stop the werewolf curse.

And yet, beneath the veneer of understanding and social empathy, the thrill of the dark creature still existed. Perhaps there is in all of us, buried deep beneath our sophisticated exteriors, a desire to return to the unfettered wild of our ancestors. The desire surfaced in society through legends and tales about werewolves, some of which finished up, as has already been mentioned, as sanitized children's stories. There were also some werewolf novels that found their way into mainstream literature, which, although they never carried the same impact as vampire works, still did much to keep the idea of the werewolf very much alive.

One of the seminal werewolf books was written by an American who wrote under the name of Samuel Guy Endore (1900–1970), although he'd been born Samuel Goldstein in New York. His 1933 book *The Werewolf of Paris* has been described by some critics as the werewolf's answer to *Dracula*, and is full of sexual tension, the eating of human flesh, and all the other elements that characterized the werewolf tale. The plot follows the life of its hero Bertrand Collet, who is the offspring of the rape of his mother by a priest (as has already been pointed out, the children of priests were invariably doomed to become werewolves), and who is born with hair on the palms of his hands,

Conclusion

as he settles in the Paris Commune of 1871. He falls in love and desperately tries to limit or even erase the "curse" that he feels himself to be under, and the story charts both his efforts to do this, as well as his love life. The book, written in some respects to compete with Stoker's *Dracula* and Mary Shelly's *Frankenstein*, is rather slow paced, and in the eyes of some reviewers, rather sloppily written. Nevertheless, the novel (with screenplay by Anthony Hinds) formed the basis of the 1961 film *Curse of the Werewolf,* directed by Terence Fisher and starring Oliver Reed and Yvonne Romain. It was made by the famous Hammer Film Studios and was filmed at Bray Studios in Berkshire. Although the script was loosely based on Endore's novel, Hinds was quick to name the book as "a classic." The film was reasonably successful, and for a while in the early 1960s, the werewolf came to the fore in the popular imagination once again.

In 1979, a collection of short stories under the title *The Bloody Chamber* propelled the werewolf into the public perception once again. Written by the English novelist and journalist Angela Carter, the stories were a modern reworking of a number of familiar childhood tales—the title story was a modern retelling of "Bluebeard"—and they contained several werewolf legends, such as *Red Riding Hood.* One of these, *A Company of Wolves* (perhaps the most direct reworking), attracted the attention of the celebrated film director Neil Jordan, who turned it into a Gothic movie, which got great acclaim when first released in 1984. It starred Sarah Patterson as an innocent girl whose slightly sinister grandmother tells her gruesome tales of heavy-browed strangers who sometimes approached young and vulnerable village maidens and carried them off into the forest, and of how wolves sometimes appeared from the darkness after these innocents had vanished. Of course, many of these handsome men were in fact fierce wolves in another form, who would ravage young girls and consume old women. This was the story of Red Riding Hood, but the film was actually about the loss of innocence and virginity. As such, it fairly dripped with sexual connections and connotations with which the wolves were associated. The movie was sumptuously filmed, and the well-written and eerily evocative script allowed all sorts of subtle themes to be developed, which drew even more interest. In fact, it was described by some critics as a "Gothic masterpiece." The acclaim that the film (and by association, Carter's book) received brought the concept of the werewolf, now with a simmering sexuality, to the fore in public imagination once again for a time

The critical success of *A Company of Wolves* (and *Wolf* 10 years later) and the ability of the werewolf theme to draw well-known directors and actors stimulated the public imagination and made the genre fairly popular throughout the 1980s and early 1990s. However, with the rise of vampire television programs and films such as *Buffy* and *Twilight*, interest in the feral man-creature appears to have fallen into abeyance once again. However, the skulking specter of the beast still hasn't gone away. It remains somewhere in our memory, ready to emerge, snarling, from the gloom. From time to time, the word *werewolf* is applied to sadistic killers who might brutalize and even sometime cannibalize their victims—killers such as, say, Jeffrey Dahmer. In former times, such killers might well have been treated much like the accused in the 16th-century French werewolf trials.

In July 1990, a serial sex attacker was jailed for a series of rapes all across the southeast of England. The *Independent* newspaper for July 3, 1990, branded him "the werewolf rapist," because several of his attacks seem to have taken place at the time of the new moon. According to reports, there was nothing especially wolf-like about the attacker's appearance—in fact, by all accounts he seemed a rather pathetic character, but the idea of a frenzied creature, controlled by bestial urges, had attached itself to his crimes. The murderer had been captured, and again, he looked nothing like a wolf, but the name had become so ingrained in the communal psyche that it stuck and was now used at random to describe brutal murderers and frenzied sexual predators.

In 1991, roughly a year after the "werewolf rapist" had been arrested, another sexual criminal—now branded as "The Wolfman" escaped from Broadmoor Psychiatric Hospital and terrorized communities in the south of England for several days before being recaptured outside a pub in Devon. He had, since his escape, been living rough on the moors in the manner of a wild beast—an image with which the newspapers had a field day. The idea of a predator, however, prowling about all over the south of England, was an incredibly potent one and evoked old fears of the beast lurking in the shadows in the minds of many ordinary people. The term *werewolf* had thus become little more than a kind of cipher used to describe such people and their socially perceived perverted ways. It was a description that tapped directly into old and deeply buried fears; such fears are indeed still with us today.

And what of the suggested connections between lycanthropy and insanity? Although he did not openly specify it, Johann Weyer hinted at a connection as far back as the 16th century. However, work in that area has been remarkably scant and boils down to just a handful of studies. In 1975, two American doctors, Dr. Frida Surawicz and Dr. Richard Banta, studied two cases of lycanthropy—one involving a 20-year-old Appalachian man with a prolonged history of drug abuse (Mr. H). After taking LSD while serving with the U.S. Army in Europe, the subject went into the woods alone where he imagined that he was turning into a wolf, and saw tufts of hair sprouting from his face and hands, which were turning into claws. Once fully transformed, he experienced an urge to hunt down and kill other animals. Back at the U.S. base, Mr. H. remained convinced that he was a werewolf and was worried that he would attack some of his fellow soldiers. He claimed to know diabolical secrets that had been shown to him while in his wolf state, although the idea of demon (wolf) possession may have arisen out of his recent viewing of the film version of William Blatty's *The Exorcist*.

It is, of course, possible to argue that the cocktail of hallucinogens with which Mr. H. bombarded his body had damaged his grip on reality, and a similar explanation can be offered for the second case study, who is referred to as Mr. W. A 30-year-old farmer, he began to grow his hair abnormally long, took to sleeping in cemeteries and howling at the moon, and believed himself to be either a wolf or some other form of canine. He also took to lying down in the street and falling asleep like a dog. On examination and comparison of notes that detailed tests taken when he had been in the U.S. Navy, it was found that Mr. W's brain was deteriorating to the point of retardation due to some form of illness. This was the likely cause of his werewolf "delusion."

Shortly after Surawicz and Banta published their finding there was another well-documented case. This involved a 49-year-old American woman, who did not actually believe she was transformed into a wolf, but began to experience urges which involved bestiality, lesbianism, and adultery (she had been married for some considerable time), which she eventually gave in to tearing off all her clothes at a family gathering and going about howling like a wolf. The next day, she savaged her husband in a fit of sexual frenzy and gnawed and scratched at the marriage bed, urinating and defecating as she did so. She was admitted to the hospital and was diagnosed as suffering from a form of schizophrenia. However, during her episodes, she claimed that she had claws and fangs and that she was a wolf-like animal—she had been possessed by a devil who had made her this way. The idea of the wolf was not far away, even in her greatly distressed state.

Conclusion

In light of this, an investigation into some former cases was carried out by the McLean Hospital in Massachusetts during the early 1980s, which reviewed some of its earlier cases that had been diagnosed as schizophrenic. They found a number of cases (12 in all) that they classed as "lycanthropy." Not all the cases fixated on wolves—although a significant number did, and characterized this by growling, snarling, and trying to bite nurses; some claimed to be other creatures, such as a bird, a gerbil, and even a rabbit, who followed around the ward for most of the day and refused to eat any meat. One patient imagined himself to be a tiger and dressed in striped clothing and grew his fingernails to abnormal lengths. The causes of many of these states, using Freudian psychotherapy, lay in repressed sexual desires. The idea of madness and werewolfery was moving away from the straightforward idea of insanity brought on by the rays of the moon.

The wolf has been with us for a long time, and it has had a profound effect on how we choose to view the world. Indeed, it has long been thought that we might somehow morph into what is perhaps our oldest enemy. But is this merely a dream of some hunter who desires the thrill of the chase and success in the field, is it the dark power of some malefic enchanter who wishes to wreak misfortune on his or her neighbors, or is it simply the delusion of some mind damaged by drugs or disease? Whatever the answer, the wolf still remains a terrifying and potent being that and one which can still send a chill along every human spine. Be careful of the dark shadow under the light at the end of the street!

Bibliography

Barber, Paul. *Vampires, Burial and Death: Folklore and Reality*. Boston, Mass.: Yale University Press, 1988.

Baring-Gould, Sabine. *The Book of Werewolves*. London: Senate Publishers, 2006.

Bavoux, F. *Bouget: Grande Juge de la terre de St. Claude*. Basancon: Local Publication, 1956.

Bettleheim, B. *The Uses of Enchantment: Meaning and Importance of Fairy Tales*. New York: Alfred Knopf, 1976.

Black, G.S. *A List of Works Relating to Lycanthropy*. New York: New York Public Library Publications, 1920.

Burkert, W. *Ancient Mystery Cults*. Cambridge, Mass.: Harvard University Press, 1987.

Burnett-Taylor, Sir Edward. *Primitive Culture*. London: Harper Torchbooks, 1873.

Curran, Dr. Bob. *Encyclopedia of the Undead*. Franklin Lakes, N.J.: New Page Books, 2006.

Dalyell, John. *The Darker Superstitions of Scotland—Illustrated from History and Practice*. Edinburgh, Scotland: Andrew Jack and Co. Printers, 1834.

Davidson, H.R.E. *Gods and Myths of Northern Europe*. New York: Penguin, 1974.

Devlin, J. *The Superstitious Mind: French Peasants and the Supernatural in the 19th Century*. Boston, Mass.: Yale University Press, 1987.

Douglas, Adam. *The Beast Within*. Edinburgh, Scotland: Chapman Publishing, 1992.

Edwards, Katherine R. ed. *Werewolves, Witches, and Wandering Spirits*. Kirksville, Mo.: Truman State University Press, 2002.

Eisler, R. *Man Into Wolf*. New Orleans, La.: Spring Books, 1950.

Frazer, Mark. *Cannibals!* London: Legend Press, 1961.

Freiberg, James. *The Long Pig: Cannibalism in a Cultural Context*. St. Petersburg, Fla.: Lighthouse Books, 1986.

Friedman, John B. *The Monstrous Races in Medieval Thought and Art*. Boston, Mass.: Harvard University Press, 1981.

Ginzberg, Carlo. *Myths, Emblems and Clues*. Santa Fe, N.M.: Radius Books, 1990.

Glut, Donald. *True Werewolves of History*. Rockville, Ma.: Sense of Wonder Press, 2004.

Guiley, Ellen. *An Encyclopaedia of Vampires, Werewolves, and other Monsters*. New York: Checkmark Books, 2005.

Hamel, Frank. *Human Animals*. London: Kessinger Publishing, 1915.

Hulstun, Barry. *Of Wolves and Men*. London: Scribners Publishing, 1978.

Keller, Otto. *Der Wolf*. Freiburg: Leipzig, 1887.

Kelly, Walter. *Curiosities of the Indo-European Tradition and Folklore*. London: Kessinger Publishing, 1868.

Kramer, H., and J. Sprenger. *The Malleus Malificarum*. London: English Translation Montague Summers, 1928.

Krauss, Salomon. *Der Wehrwulf*. Freiburg: Leipzig, 1908.

𝔅ibliography

Lane, Harlan. *The Wild Boy of Aveyron*. Melbourne, Australia: Allen & Unwin, 1977.

Maclean, Charles. *The Wolf Children*. London: Allen Lane Publishers, 1977.

McCullough, Sir Edgar. *Guernsey Folklore*. New York: Allen Sutton Publishing, 1903.

McNally, R. *Irish Wonder Tales*. Dublin: White and Company, 1896.

O'Donnell, Elliot. *Werewolves—A Monograph*. London, 1912.

Ray, Anthony. *Wolf Children*. Orlando, Fla.: Harcourt Press, 1980.

Robbins, Russell. *Encyclopaedia of Witchcraft and Demonology*. New York: Harper Collins, 1963.

Russell, Jeffrey B. *A History of Witchcraft: Sinners, Heretics and Pagans*. London: Thames and Hudson, 1980.

Scribe, Eugene. *Le Loup Garou*. Paris: Private Publication,1827.

Senn, Harry A. *Were-wolf and Vampire in Romania*. Boulder, Colo.: University of, Colorado, 1982.

Summers, Montague. *The Werewolf in Lore and Legend*. London: Kegan Paul Publishers, 1933.

Tannahill, R. *Flesh and Blood: A History of the Cannibal Complex*. London: Hamish Hamilton, 1975.

Thomas, Keith. *Man And the Natural World: Changing Attitudes in England 1500-1800*. London: Allen Lane, 1983.

Weyer, J. "Witches, Devils, and Doctors in the Renaissance" in *Medieval and Renaissance Texts and Studies* 1991.

Wynter, Andrew. *Werewolves and Lycanthropy in Fruit Between the Leaves*. London: Chapman and Hall, 1875.

Index

Adam of Bremen, 46

Alexander the Great, 40

Angroboda, 31

animalistic spirits, 18

anthropophagi, 27

Anubis, 29-30, 85

Arcadia, 24-26

Aristodemus, 61

Artaxerxes II, 44

Artemis, 177

Assena, 186

Aztec peoples, 130

Babylon, 83

Baring-Gold, Reverend Sabine, 54

Bate Yele, the, 78

bear worship, 84

beast-man, 121, 136, 150

Beni Chelib, the, 43

Bernardino of Sienna, 75

berserkers, 56-64, 66, 100

Bidel, Bonoit, 146

Big Peter, 142-143

Bisclavret, 101-110

boanthropy, 68

Bodin, Jean, 74

Boguet, Henri, 135, 148-149

Bourgot, Pierre, 142-143, 146

Brothers Grimm, the, 162

Cambrensis, Giraldus, 93, 97, 99-100, 114, 116, 121

Campbell,
John, 106
Joseph, 20

cannibalism, 38, 40-41, 51, 78, 90, 122-133,

cannibalistic
feasts, 186
tendencies, 63

cannibals, 27, 29, 45, 47

Carnophales, 41

caul, being born with a, 183

Charcot, Jean Martin, 183-184

Chinese legend, 48-49

Christie, Andrew, 129

coyote, the, 87

CuCuhullain, 62

Cynocephali, 41-43, 45, 48

demonology, 148

Devil's Sabbat, the, 143, 145, 148

Devil-worshipers, 148

Dionysus, 69

djinn, 86

dog-headed
race, the, 40-49
saints, 38, 40

dog-heads, 91

Donners, the, 131-133

eigi einhamr, 54, 56, 70, 86

Endore, Samuel Guy, 208

Enkidu, 68

Faustulus, 21

Fenrir, 31-32

feral
attributes, 19
children, 188, 190, 193, 197
creatures, 185-198

Feronia, 26-27

fox
shrines, 50
spirits, 50

foxes, Japanese, 49-51

Freud, Sigmund, 181-183

Freya, 56

Fu Hsi, 48-49

full moons, 170-179

Gandillion, Perenette, 146

Gandillions, the, 146-149, 181

Garnier, Gilles, 139-142, 144, 162, 164

garwolf, 104, 108

Gevaudon, Bete de, 157-158

Gilgamesh, 23-24

Giovanni de Pian dei Carine, 46

Gleipnir, 31-32

Goldstein, Samuel, 208

Gorlagon, 109, 114

Grenier, Jean, 151-154, 156-158, 161-162, 164-165, 181

guerrillas, 67

Guillaume de Palerne, 114-116

Guinefort, 34-36

hallucinations, 180

Herodotus, 27, 69

Index

human sacrifice, 26-27, 78

humoral balance, the, 171-172

Indian
 legends, 33
 tribes, 130

Irish
 beasts, 62-63
 wolfhound, the, 94

kallohonka, 84-85

Kamala and Amala, 193-196

King Arthur, 106, 109

Ktesias, 44-45

kyrokephaloi, 45

Laestrygonians, 47

Laignech Faelad, the, 62, 100

leechcraft, 173

Leopard
 Cult, the, 79-80
 Men, 76-82, 84

lion cults, 82-84

Lion Man, a, 84

Llewellyn the Great, 36

loup-garou, 142

lunar
 goddess, triple, 177
 phases, 170

Luperca, 21

lycanthropes, 146, 151

lycanthropy, 149, 154, 157, 169, 201

Lykaon, 24-26

man-calf, 118

man-goat, 148

man-ox, 117

Marie de France, 101

Marmaritae, the, 36

Melion, 104-110

metempsychosis, 98-99

moon goddesses, 177

Mount Soracte, 27

Murray, Margaret, 20

Native American
 beliefs, 201
 civilization, 32-34
 tribes, 130

nature spirits, 19

nawals, 86

Nordic gods, 56

Norse, the, 61

Norse mythology, 31

Odin, 56-57

Pausanius, 25-26

Pendle witches, the, 75

Perrault, Charles, 158, 161, 163

Peter of Hanover, 192-193

Pliny, 25-27, 40

possession, 60

primal forests, 17

proto-men, 17

Queen of Sheba, 83

Ragnarok, 31-32

Romulus and Remus, 21-23, 185

Rostegny, Pierre de, 150

Roulet, Jacques, 144-145

Sabbat, witch's, 148

Sabbats, 75, 168

Sasquatch, the, 68

Satanic transformations, 75-76

Satyricon, the, 24

Sawney Bean, 122-129

Scott, Reginald, 169-170

Selene, 171, 177

Set, the serpent god, 30

shaman, 19-20, 84

shamanism, 85

shamanistic ritual, 61

shape changers, 56-57

shapeshifter, 59, 86, 88-91

she-wolf, 21, 186-188

Shoshone folklore, 33

Siculus, Diodorus, 83

silver bullet, a, 200

Silvia, Rhea, 21

skinwalkers, 88-89

skinwalking, 90

Soranian Wolves, the, 26

Sorcerer de Trois Freres, 19-21

spirit guide, 34

St. Albeus, 187

St. Andrew Cynocephali, 38

St. Bartholomew, 38

St. Christopher, 36-38, 40-43

St. Gelert, 35

St. Michael, 43

Stubbe, Peter, 136-139, 141

Thomas of Cantimpre, 46

totem poles, 33

transubstantiation, 99

Tyr, 31-32, 57

Verdung, Michael, 142-143, 146

Viking lawmakers, 64

Vincent of Beauvais, 46

Voodoo, 130, 201

Walter of Speyer, 37

Werewolf Brigade, the, 202

werewolfery, 141-142, 155, 164-165, 170, 184

werewolfism, 179

Weyer, Dr. Johann, 164-165, 167-170, 180

Wild Boy of Aveyron, the, 188, 190-192

William I, 65

witch doctor, 84-85

witchcraft, 71, 74, 76, 88, 138, 148-49, 154, 164, 168-170, 180, 184

witchcraft trials, 167

witches, 71-73, 75, 89, 148, 150, 168, 184

witch-hunter, 150

witch-hunts, 73-75

wodewose, 67-68

Wolf

    Girls of Godamuri, the, 193-196

    Man, the, 182

    Master, the, 182-183

wolf skins, 19

wolfsbane, 181, 184

woodwose, 67-68, 70

xenophobia, 29

About the Author

Dr. Bob Curran was born in a remote area of County Down, Northern Ireland. The area in which he grew up was rich in folklore—especially the folklore of the supernatural—and this gave him an ear for and an interest in the tales and beliefs of many people. He has worked in a number of jobs before going to university, where he took a doctorate in child psychology. Even so, his interest in folklore and folk culture was still very much in the fore, and this prompted him to write a number of books on the subject, including *Celtic Lord and Legend*; *Vampires*; and *Lost Lands, Forgotten Realms*. Having taken another degree in history, he now lectures and broadcasts on matters of historical interest, and acts as advisor to a number of influential cultural bodies in Northern Ireland. Most recently he has been working on advisory bodies regarding cultural links between Northern Ireland and the West of Scotland. He currently lives in Northern Ireland with his wife and young family.